THE VIRTUE OF YIN

Studies on Chinese Women

Lily Xiao Hong Lee

Published by WILD PEONY PTY LTD ACN 002 714 276
PO Box 636 Broadway NSW 2007 Australia
Fax 61 2 566 1052

International Distribution:
University of Hawaii Press, 2480 Kolowalu Street, Honolulu
Hawaii 96822
Fax 1 808 988 6052

First published 1994

ISBN 0 646 14925 3

Printed in Australia by National Capital Printing, Canberra

THE VIRTUE OF YIN
Studies on Chinese Women

Lily Xiao Hong Lee

wild peony

We acknowledge the assistance of the University of Sydney in the publication of this volume.

To My Mother Long Yee

Acknowledgements

This thin volume represents a portion of my research over recent years. Several of the chapters have been published in journals and the others presented at conferences.

I acknowledge with thanks permission to reprint from *Mingbao yuekan* and *The Journal of the Oriental Society of Australia*. "Xie Daoyun: The Style of a Woman *Mingshi*" was published in *Mingbao yuekan*, No. 217 (January 1984). "The Emergence of Buddhist Nuns in China" was published in *The Journal of the Oriental Society of Australia*, Vols 18-19 (1986-87).

"Ban Zhao (c. 48-c. 120): Her Role in the Formulation of Controls Imposed Upon Women in Traditional China" was presented at the Sixth Biennial Conference of the Asian Studies Association of Australia held at the Australian National University in February 1988. "Where are the Heroines of the Long March Now? A Survey of Their Lives and Work After 1949" was presented at the "China: Forty Years After" Conference held at the University of Sydney in September 1989. "Helen Quach's Work With East and Southeast Asian Symphony Orchestras" was presented at the "New Directions in Asian Studies" Conference which was jointly organized by the Asian Studies Association of Australia and the National University of Singapore and held in Singapore in February 1989.

I would like to thank my colleague Mabel Lee for her support and encouragement throughout the years. To my friend Kate Kerr I would like to offer a special word of thanks; she was often the first reader of many of my papers, and her patience and valuable suggestions are greatly appreciated. To my husband and my three daughters I am also indebted; I imposed on them to read the manuscript while we were on holidays.

Most importantly, I am grateful to the University of Sydney for providing a grant to assist the publication of this volume.

Finally, my gratitude goes to Professor Liu Weiping whose calligraphy adds so much elegance to the cover of this book.

L. L.
University of Sydney
June 1994

CONTENTS

Introduction

Mao Zedong once said that "Women hold up half of the sky". This metaphor, derived from the ancient Chinese mythology in which the goddess Nüwa was said to have propped up the sky in order to save it from falling, graphically portrays an ideal situation in which men and women share equal responsibility in the affairs of the world.

What exactly has been the position of women in China, both traditional and modern? A contradictory picture presents itself. On the one hand, we can cite the oppressive customs and atrocious treatment which aimed to keep women in servitude or to make them the playthings of men. On the other hand, we can point to women such as Ban Zhao, Xie Daoyun, Li Qingzhao, Ding Ling and a handful of other women scholars and writers, and say that it was possible for women in China to receive a good education and become accomplished and well respected in their respective fields. We can point to Hua Mulan, a legendary figure who became popular in the Northern Dynasties (386-581), and to other women army commanders after her whose exploits are based on more solid historical evidence—women such as Liang Hongyu and Qin Liangyu, as well as the women in the Red Army—and maintain that Chinese women also have a reputation for being good soldiers. We can also point to Empress Wu, Empress Cixi, Xishi and Yang Guifei, the Soong sisters, Jiang Qing, and conclude that they exerted great influence on Chinese politics and were critical figures in Chinese history.

However, as in the rest of the world, compared with the thousands of men in Chinese history who have achieved fame for political, scholarly or military achievements, virtue, influence or even for their shortcomings or crimes, the number of women who have made themselves known to posterity is pathetically small. Perhaps it was because in traditional China for women to be distinguished was to violate the code of modest behaviour. For such conduct women could be made to suffer hardship, loneliness and isolation, provided they were fortunate enough to escape the worse fate of open vilification and humiliation. It seems that those women who became well known in traditional China did so not as a result of their own aspirations but in spite of themselves. Hence it is not surprising that so few of them are known to us now. What has been transmitted to us today about their lives is even more limited.

Generally speaking, in China there are two conditions which have allowed women to achieve some degree of immortality. The first required that women be born into specific family milieus. Women born into scholar-official families were far more likely to receive an education. They were also more likely to be free of the labour of production and housework and hence to have the leisure to pursue academic, literary or artistic interests. The talented and seriously

1

committed ones had the possibility of becoming well known in their endeavours. In Chinese literature and art, many women writers and artists are wives, sisters and daughters of well-known male artists and writers. Even in the martial arts, we can find examples of women warriors and generals who were trained by a father or husband. The legendary Hua Mulan's father must have been a well-known soldier, or else his name would not have appeared on every volume that contained the names of military personnel called to battle. Liang Hongyu was the daughter of an officer stationed at the border. She had been trained in the martial arts since childhood. Later she became the wife of Han Shizhong, one of the famous generals of the Southern Song dynasty, and helped him in his military career.[1] Similarly, Qin Liangyu, later to be appointed by the Ming Court as Military Governor of Shizhu (modern Sichuan), was the daughter of an expert on military strategy and she and all her brothers were trained from childhood in riding, archery and the art of war.[2] However, it must be assumed that one other factor was crucial to a woman's success besides talent, leisure and commitment: if the male members of their families were not sympathetic, they would not have been allowed to utilize their talents and leisure as they chose. Pastimes such as sewing and embroidery would certainly have been deemed by most fathers and husbands as more suitable feminine pursuits. Only when the men were tolerant or encouraged such activities could talented and hard-working women hope to achieve any degree of accomplishment.

Ironically, women from very poor families seem to have had a better chance of achieving fame, usually under abnormal circumstances. Women of the very poor were not required to endure the restrictions imposed upon middle and upper class women, such as not being able to venture outside the family home or to talk to strange men. They had to work in the fields, pick mulberry leaves or gather firewood in the wilderness and consequently could not avoid contact with the outside world. As a result of the physical nature of their work they were strong and fit and when their richer sisters had bound feet, the feet of peasant women stayed in their natural state. When, from time to time the peasants of China were driven to insurrection, it was not unusual for women to join in taking up arms against the government of the time. Women took part in several Daoist insurrections from the Han dynasty to the Jin dynasty. In the early Ming dynasty a woman leader of the White Lotus Sect named Tang Sai'er in 1420 led an insurrection which lasted several months and involved several counties in Shandong province, even threatening the capital.[3] Her story is told in fiction in *Nüxian waishi*. Closer to our own times we find women in the ranks

---

[1] *Song shi*, j. 364, p. 11361, 11365.
[2] *Qin Liangyu shiliao jicheng*, p. 10.
[3] See *Ming shi*, j. 7, p. 99, and also Lü Xiong, *Nüxian waishi*.

of the Taipings and Boxers. Peasant women also joined the Red Army and became leaders of the Chinese Communist Party.

The second condition is related to social milieu. In Chinese society, women were normally under fairly tight control in the past. Even up to modern times, the force of conservatism still often rears its head. Under such circumstances, women have little chance of transcending their own inertia developed over centuries of inculcation to obedience and mediocrity, let alone the written or unwritten constraints placed upon them by men. Only in very specific situations in which these constraints were temporarily absent or at least relaxed could women be inspired, sometimes driven, to strive for excellence or even to take up roles which were traditionally considered masculine. This applied when women belonged to groups outside the normal Chinese social structure, for example, when they were members of religious groups (Buddhist or Daoist orders) or were social outcasts (actresses and courtesans). Since such women had divorced themselves from the family, Confucian social norms were no longer applied with the same rigour to their activities. Constraints on women were also relaxed during periods of total social upheaval when all the old values were uprooted and new ones had not yet been established. During such extraordinary periods women were able to engage in many unusual activities: fighting in wars, taking part in revolutions, managing public affairs and sometimes even ruling a nation.

There is no evidence to confirm that women enjoyed equal rights with men before the Han dynasty, but from Liu Xiang's *Lienü zhuan* as well as some pre-Han historical texts it can be seen that women were praised for their intelligence, independence of mind, and their achievements as well as their feminine virtue. It is possible to say that while women were not actively encouraged to excel, they were not actively discouraged from doing so.

The phenomenon of Ban Zhao can serve to illustrate this point. In her own time, i.e., in the first century A.D., it was still possible for a woman to attain great heights. She was born into a privileged scholar-official family and enjoyed an excellent education, even by male standards. None of the constraints she later recommended for other women seem to have been placed upon her. Instead of being discouraged from her endeavours, she was repeatedly honoured and rewarded for them. It would appear that, though there were already certain views at the time on how women should behave, they had not yet been coordinated into a comprehensive set of codes, and these uncoordinated views were only loosely observed. Thus Ban Zhao was not only able to become a great historian and teacher, but had the rare opportunity of participating in the political decision-making of the Court through her pupil, Dowager Empress Deng. She became the embodiment of the ideal woman, who brought honour and benevolence to her own family and also to her husband's family.

Yet it was precisely during the time when Ban Zhao was engaged in the activities which would bring her fame that a tide of conservatism swept Eastern Han China. This conservatism was responsible for a body of writing that shaped Chinese opinion for centuries to come.[4] A number of Confucian scholars, including Liu Xiang, Ban Zhao and her brother Ban Gu, saw a need to formulate a comprehensive set of rites to govern social behaviour. For them, Chinese society had gone through a long period of moral decline from the ideal of the Zhou dynasty when people behaved according to the rites as formulated by the Duke of Zhou. The intervening centuries were characterized by chaos, both political and moral. Even worse, with the burning of books in the preceding Qin dynasty, the Han people had lost the very basis for restoring the ideal state. According to them, a comprehensive set of rites needed to be constructed to guide the people.[5] Possibly it was due to this belief that Ban Zhao wrote her *Nüjie* (Precepts for women). This work had a highly negative influence on the education and development of women in traditional China. On the surface, Ban Zhao displayed a positive attitude towards the education of women and advocated that all women should receive an education. However, at the same time, she advocated that women's learning should be confined to didactic texts and to the simple skills necessary for managing a household. Furthermore, her book attempted to restrict women's freedom of movement by re-emphasizing that they should not venture outside the house or communicate with people other than those of their own family.

Probably the factor most detrimental to women's achievements in the centuries to come was the discouraging of women from excellence by inculcating the importance of modesty and humility. Attitudes as late as Liu Xiang's, as reflected in his *Lienü zhuan*, had been in favour of women speaking their own minds and distinguishing themselves intellectually as well as morally. The change in attitude that was advocated by Ban Zhao, while enabling many women to receive a basic education, in fact restricted the range of their activities and stifled their creativity. Ban Zhao's historical stature perhaps speaks eloquently for the effectiveness of her teaching. She has always been extolled as the most erudite woman in Chinese history. It has only been in modern times that reference has been made to the negative influence she has had on the lives of Chinese women. A thorough investigation is needed to assess the effect of her influence which, though it did not apparently bring about an immediate change in the lives of women after her, nevertheless intensified later in the favourable climate of Neo-Confucianism. My paper on Ban Zhao focuses on her role of

---

[4] Jack Dull, "Marriage and Divorce in Han China: a Glimpse at 'Pre-Confucian' Society", David C. Buxbaum, *Chinese Family Law and Social Change: In Historical and Comparative Perspective*, pp. 36-8.
[5] *Ibid.*

consolidating existing precepts and attitudes toward women into a systematic, comprehensive code of precepts in her *Nüjie*.

The influence of Confucianism on Chinese society was not uniform through the ages; there were periods in Chinese history during which the force of tradition was weaker. It was usually in these periods that women were freed from the restrictions which tradition had placed on them and given the opportunity to develop themselves more fully. However even during these periods of relative freedom, only the more privileged women born into élite families could benefit from such temporary relaxation. The poor could not hope to enjoy any respite from the limitations placed on them by poverty.

Xie Daoyun was born during such a period of reduced control and into an élite family which dictated trends rather than followed them. Her story demonstrates to us how a woman was able to fulfil her potential during such rare periods in Chinese history when individualism was praised and not suppressed. She was able to stretch the rules to an amazing degree but the fact that she was unique, even in her own time, makes it apparent that very few women could hope to emulate her. By delineating her historical milieu, her family background, her talent and her ability, the paper on Xie Daoyun shows how it was a chance combination of factors which produced this singular, remarkable women.

It has been pointed out that often at the beginning of a mass movement, all followers, male or female, were welcomed, because of the initial hardship involved and the doubtful future of the movement. During this less organized stage, women were often able to attain high positions.[6] However, as the movement gained support and strength, and a tighter organization was established, women were gradually discarded or relegated to the lower end of the organization's hierarchy. Both the early Buddhist nuns in China and the women of the Long March seem to confirm that this tendency has continued into modern times.

When Buddhism was introduced to China in the Wei-Jin period, followers were few as no organized institutions existed at the time. Women with initiative, like Jingjian and her colleagues, established and developed their own convents without even knowing the exact rules and regulations. The resistance to their innovative action was formidable: they risked being disowned by their families and persecuted by officials. Yet they persisted and began to win the respect and admiration of the nobility and common people alike. The convents opened many avenues in Chinese intellectual as well as social life. One of these was to offer women an alternative to the traditional role of wife and mother. It also offered them complete independence from men. For the first time a woman could, if she preferred, be identified as an

---

[6] Michel Perrot *et al.*, "A propos du destin de la femme XVIe au XXe siècle", Evalyn Sullerot (ed.), *Le Fait feminin*, p. 439.

individual and not merely as someone's wife or mother; in addition a woman was provided with an escape route from an unhappy home when she had trouble with her husband or in-laws. The intellectually inclined could pursue knowledge and enlightenment with the help of a wide range of Buddhist scholars in the field, regardless of gender. A woman could preach and teach openly and her achievements could be publicly recognized. The more practical nuns could find satisfaction in managing the business side of the convents which were often large establishments housing hundreds of people. They could even plan for future expansion by embarking on building programs. The most ambitious women found it possible to influence the affairs of the state through their patrons, among whom they could count emperors and prime ministers. Due to the unprecedented freedom which they enjoyed in the early period, many distinguished nuns emerged.

The paper on the emergence of the Buddhist nuns traces the beginning of the Buddhist convents and the lives and activities of the early nuns through the *Biqiuni zhuan* and other Buddhist as well as secular sources. It also attempts to discover what women were able to find in the alternative life offered by religious orders. The divergent interests of the thirteen nuns surveyed reveal the scope of their talents and efforts. Their achievements in various fields of endeavour also served as an incentive for women who followed. Yet we find few of their calibre from the Tang dynasty onwards. The reason for this is complex and includes such factors as the lowering of the integrity of the nuns themselves. However, the sinicization of Buddhism, which brought the Buddhist community back within the influence of Confucian patriarchal thinking, certainly played an important part.

It has generally been accepted by scholars of Chinese women's studies that Neo-Confucianism brought an escalation and tightening of the degree of control placed on women. Precepts which had so far only been loosely observed started to be enforced more rigourously. With the Ming dynasty, a succession of texts for women appeared, modelled on Ban Zhao's *Nüjie*. The Neo-Confucian pathological emphasis on *jie*, chastity, created strong public sanctions against widows re-marrying and encouraged widow suicide. It has been maintained that the saying "Being untalented is a virtue in a woman" did not appear before the Ming dynasty.[7] Coincidentally, the popularity of foot-binding seems to have gained momentum roughly in the Ming-Qing period when the social customs and attitudes inspired by Neo-Confucianism were carried to extremes.

However, a concurrent development in the other direction also took place in this period. With the advances made in printing, books became more readily accessible. Consequently, in addition to the emergence of an educated middle class, there was an easier transmission of learning

---

[7] Chen Dongyuan, *Zhongguo funü shenghuo shi*, p. 188.

from the male members of a family to its female members. With books in the home, a girl who was so inclined could almost teach herself to read. In time, a chain of transmission established itself by which knowledge was passed between female members of a family, e.g. from mother to daughter, aunt to niece, sister to sister, cousin to cousin, mistress to maid. This would account for the proliferation of women writers and poets in the Ming-Qing period despite the pervasiveness of the Neo-Confucian attitude that "being untalented is a virtue in a woman".

From the sixteenth and seventeenth centuries, perhaps as a reaction to the irrational and often cruel customs of the time, a sprinkling of male Chinese scholars, such as Lü Kun and Yuan Mei, expressed sympathy for the lot of women.[8] They were followed by a small group of more outspoken scholars who expressed concepts relating to the equality of the sexes and who called for reform in the treatment of women. It should be noted that these developments occurred independently of any Western influence.

When China opened its doors to Western technology in the nineteenth century, it received as a side effect Western social and political ideas as well. One of them was feminism. Male reformists such as Kang Youwei and Liang Qichao recognized the need to change the treatment of women, especially such extreme and cruel customs as foot-binding and widow suicide. They also recognized the need to educate women so that they could make a greater contribution to the strengthening of China. It is difficult to ascertain whether Kang and Liang had the benefit of women in mind when advocating the liberation of women. They certainly did not argue from a humanitarian point of view; their concerns were based on benefiting the country. They argued that if the energies of women, half the nation's population, were liberated and enlisted in production, the increase would help to make China richer. If Chinese women continued to be ignorant and superstitious, the children they raised would never be the kind of citizens who could build a stronger China.[9] At the turn of the century, women students returning from Japan and graduates of Western missionary schools at home joined the fight against the oppression of women; they went further and demanded equal rights. Yet to many women of that period, with Qiu Jin as their most illustrious representative, feminism was still tightly bound to patriotism.[10] In

---

[8] Paul S. Ropp, "The Seeds of Change: Reflections on the Conditions of Women in the Early and Mid Ch'ing," *Signs*, No. 2, 1976, pp. 5-23; and "Women in Men's Eyes: *Ju-lin wai-shih* and Feminist Thought" in his *Dissent in Early Modern China*, Chapter IV.

[9] Catherine Gipolon, "The Emergence of Women in Politics in China, 1898-1927", *Chinese Studies in History* (Winter 1989/90), p. 48.

[10] Charlotte Beahan, "Feminism and Nationalism in the Chinese Women's Press, 1902-1911", *Modern China* (1975), pp. 379-416.

fact, the two issues were in effect inseparable. This attitude prevailed among women during at least the first half of the twentieth century. The beginning of the Communist movement in China only strengthened women's convictions about both of these issues.

Women in the Communist camp added the further issue of class struggle. Marxism encouraged women to throw themselves into the torrent against social oppression and to fight for their own liberation while liberating the oppressed masses.[11] Among the earliest members of the Chinese Communist Party were women such as Xiang Jingyu, Cai Chang, Deng Yingchao and Zhang Qinqiu who put this concept into action. They provided leadership to the Chinese women in the Communist Party, the women workers in Shanghai and the peasant women in the soviets. They fought side by side with their male counterparts in various fields, showing great courage and resourcefulness. Wherever they went, women followed their example. In the countryside where the lot of women was the hardest, women responded more readily to Communist propaganda. When most of the able-bodied men were needed for fighting, the peasant women shouldered the lion's share of the responsibility for production. It is ironic that Mao Zedong, who would have considered himself far more progressive than Kang Youwei, seems to have shared Kang's interest in the economic value of liberating Chinese women. He said, "Chinese women are a great human resource. We must excavate this resource for our struggle to build a great socialist nation."[12] This was a major reason for both Mao and the Party placing women's work on a very high level of priority. By the time the Long March began, a group of highly committed women party members already existed.

The women who took part in the Long March were, in general, from two social classes: the scholar-official class and the poor peasants. The former, mostly educated women, joined the Communist movement for idealistic reasons. For most of the latter group, however, it was a fight for survival. Like the women who participated in various other rebellions throughout the history of China, they took this action because they saw no alternative. For both groups, their cause was so compelling that they were able to accomplish what has been described as the most gruelling odyssey of modern times.[13] However, due to the secrecy in which the Chinese Communist Party kept the lives of people under their rule, especially the lives of their leaders, the story of the Long March women remained virtually unknown to the world until recent times. During the 1980s portraits of some of these women were

---

[11] Li Xiaojiang, *Xiawa de tansuo*, p. 24.

[12] Mao Zedong, *Mao Zedong xuanji*, Vol. 5, p. 252.

[13] A statement by Edgar Snow quoted in D. Wilson's *The Long March, 1935: the Epic of Chinese Communism's Survival*, p. xvi.

published,[14] but only the most prominent among them are known to the West.

What happened to the heroines who endured so much in order to help the Chinese Communists gain power is of even greater interest. They had fought so selflessly to realize their ideals, but were they given a share of the satisfying work of reconstructing China after the revolution? The paper on the life and work of the Long March women after 1949 endeavours to provide an outline, however sketchy and incomplete, of this heretofore unexplored subject. It surveys the personal and familial background of the women, their education and work experience before the Long March, as well as their experiences during the Long March. Special effort has been given to finding out information about their marriage partner or partners, although sometimes this was not an easy task. For information on the early life of some of these women, works by foreign writers such as Edgar and Helen (Nym Wales) Snow, Agnes Smedley and Harrison Salisbury have not only been important, but sometimes indispensable. On their lives after 1949, in most cases only formal biographical data containing official titles have been available; such sources seldom provide much insight into their actual work and the responsibility attached to their positions.

From the eighteenth century, large numbers of Chinese people from the coastal provinces, especially Guangdong and Fujian, began to migrate to Southeast Asia. In the mid-twentieth century, after generations of subsistence living, the overseas Chinese began to enjoy the fruits of their labour. Some have made fortunes in their adopted countries, but the majority, who could only be described as leading comfortable lives, are already beginning to divert part of their their energies and material wealth to cultural pursuits. The overseas Chinese communities in Western countries inevitably absorbed Western cultural influences and adopted the evolving attitudes of the societies of which they had become an integral part. Of revelance here was the development of a more open attitude towards women in the West and the entry of women into professions traditionally monopolized by men. By the mid-twentieth century an Asian female orchestra conductor of Western music appeared in the person of Helen Quach.

Helen Quach was born of Chinese parents in French-ruled Vietnam. Her parents, who were second generation Vietnamese Chinese, not only broke tradition by investing all their attention on a daughter, but also chose for her the conventionally lowly placed profession of music. Instead of the safer and less complicated options of studying to be a vocalist or instrumentalist she chose to become a symphony conductor. She was faced with the double handicap of being a woman in a male-dominated profession and being an Asian in the world of Western

---

[14] See Liaowang Bianjibu, *Hongjun nüyingxiong zhuan* and entries in various biographical dictionaries published since the mid-1980s.

music. Though lauded as being as talented as any male conductor, if not better than most, Quach found that she was generally only able to find work in East and Southeast Asia where symphony orchestras were still in a fledgling stage of development. This meant that she was not able to enjoy and develop a professional career unhampered by more mundane worries. The paper on Helen Quach's work with East and Southeast Asian orchestras was written to examine how a hybrid of Eastern and Western cultures developed in Asian societies, and to evaluate her contribution to orchestras in the region.

The women discussed in this book lived at various times in history, from the first century to the twentieth century, and they came from very different family backgrounds: from poor peasant families, from the most honoured scholar-official families, and from middle-class merchant families. Their fields of accomplishment also differed widely: historiography, moral education, literature, philosophy, religion, political struggle and Western music. Geographically, aside from the coastal region, and the valleys of the Yellow and Yangtze Rivers which are the most populous parts of China, they also came from the arid northwest and the jungles of the southwest. One subject is an overseas Chinese brought up outside China. If we are to look for something common to all of them, it would be found in the fact that they all challenged tradition and played a role which was not normally that of a woman. Theirs was a tortuous and rough road. Difficulties, often seemingly insurmountable, lay in their paths. To be acknowledged in their fields they needed to be better than their male counterparts. Furthermore, since society traditionally punished those who dared to be different, only the lucky ones were able to escape vilification and being ostracized. Hence exceptional courage, endurance and perseverance were qualities common to all of these women.

Throughout China's long history, only the lives of a few very distinguished women have been documented in any detail. The reality of women's life is still largely uncharted territory. History has hitherto only been concerned with the activities of men. In recent decades people of all cultures have been consciously trying to fill in that half of history which is virtually blank, the half which concerns women, and which is missing from conventional history. It is hoped that the following pages will serve as a few bricks in the construction of "the other half" of Chinese history.

Ban Zhao (c. 48-c. 120): Her Role in the Formulation of Controls Imposed Upon Women in Traditional China

The name of Ban Zhao or Cao *dagu* has been invoked for centuries as a model for young girls to emulate. Even modern scholars, both Chinese and Western, have lauded her achievements as historian, educator, writer and moralist. Despite the introduction of Western feminist thought to China at the turn of this century, Xie Wuliang, in his *Zhongguo funü wenxueshi*[1] (1917) does not comment on her important role in the formulation of the detailed rules by which women's thought and behaviour were controlled in traditional China. During the May Fourth period, one of the strongest anti-Confucian forces was directed at the eradication of inequalities between the sexes and the shattering of the many forms of control imposed on women, yet no organized criticism of Ban Zhao for her role in formulating such controls appears in that period. Though, in his *Zhongguo funü shenghuo shi* (1937), Chen Dongyuan gives a brief critique on Ban Zhao's views regarding women and puts her in the correct perspective,[2] and Tienchi Martin-Liao, in her more recent study (1984) on the education of Chinese women, points to a connection between Ban Zhao's elevated position at court and her Confucian outlook, and to her conservative stance on the question of equality between men and women,[3] these views have yet to be fully substantiated.

In 1932, Nancy Lee Swann, whose study of Ban Zhao is perhaps still by far the most comprehensive and detailed to date, recognized her as the first thinker to formulate a single complete statement of feminine ethics,[4] thus re-affirming her positive image in the history of Chinese women, rather than giving her a critical re-appraisal from a modern and progressive viewpoint. The following quotation may serve to show Swann's own outlook on the relationship between men and women:

> The feminine virtues are immutable, and what is required by modern conditions is a restatement rather than a rejection of Pan Chao's instructions.[5]

It is obvious that she agrees with the basic tenets advocated by Ban Zhao: that man is superior to woman and obedience should be the guiding principle of a woman's behaviour throughout her life. It is the

---

[1] Xie Wuliang, *Zhongguo funü wenxueshi*, Section 2, pp. 18-28.
[2] Chen Dongyuan, *Zhongguo funü shenghuo shi*, p. 47.
[3] Tienchi Martin-Liao, *Frauenerziehung im Alten China, eine Analyse der Frauenbücher*, p. 50.
[4] Nancy Lee Swann, *Pan Chao: Foremost Woman Scholar of China, First Century A.D.*, p. 133.
[5] Swann, *op. cit.*, p. 138.

purpose of this paper to re-evaluate Ban Zhao's role in formulating standards which were used later to impose control over women.

Among Ban Zhao's works, *Nüjie* (Precepts for women) is the one that deals with this subject. She wrote it when she was more than fifty-four and had reached the zenith of her career.[6] Her professed motive for writing it was to give guidance to "my girls" who were about to be married, so that they would know how to behave when they went into their husband's families. Assuming, for the moment, that that was her genuine motive, it is possible that she also intended it to be used by girls in general. In Chapter II of *Nüjie,* Ban Zhao advocates education for girls between the ages of eight and fifteen. Perhaps she had intended that *Nüjie* should act as a sort of primer for girls, thereby combining reading and moral education in the one textbook.

Nüjie was not the first work to aim at the moral edification of women.[7] Liu Xiang wrote *Lienü zhuan* (Biography of eminent women) because he thought that the palace women of the Western Han came from lowly origins and, not having had proper education, were guilty of improper behaviour.[8] The *Lienü zhuan* consists of the biographies of one hundred and twenty five women, arranged into categories ranging from "virtuous and wise" to "pernicious and depraved". Ban Zhao's work, however, is probably the more complete and systematic. It begins by stating the Confucian tenet that man is superior and woman is inferior and proceeds to counsel women to accept it as an underlying principle for behaviour and social relationships. Further, Ban Zhao provides specific instructions on a woman's personal conduct and the way in which a woman should behave in relationships with her husband and members of his family.

The entire text of *Nüjie* is found in Ban Zhao's biography in the *Hou Han shu.*[9] As far as I know, there are three complete English translations—one in Swann's book,[10] one in Florence Ayscough's *Chinese Women Yesterday and Today,*[11] and a third by van Gulik which appears in his *Sexual Life in Ancient China.*[12] A German translation is also available in Martin-Liao's book mentioned above.[13]

---

[6] In her "Introduction" to *Nüjie* Ban Zhao stated that it was more than forty years since she had married into the Cao family at the age of fourteen.

[7] Ban Zhao refers to another work entitled *Nü xian* (Rules for women) which was possibly also for the education of women. Swann claims that Liang Qichao and Gu Jiegang both told her that they thought it to be a long lost book. See Swann, *op. cit.,* p. 97, note 31.

[8] *Han shu,* j. 36, p. 1957.

[9] *Hou Han shu,* j. 84, p. 2786-92.

[10] Swann, *op. cit.,* pp. 86-99.

[11] Florence Ayscough, *Chinese Women Yesterday and Today,* pp. 237-49.

[12] Robert van Gulik, *Sexual Life in Ancient China: a Preliminary Survey of Chinese Sex and Society from 1500 B.C. to 1644 A.D.*

[13] Martin-Liao, *op. cit.,* pp. 95-110.

Swann, and no doubt many others, was of the opinion that *Nüjie* is Ban Zhao's interpretation of classical teaching concerning women and the family, and that she merely inherits and expounds what was taught before her. However, close scrutiny of her precepts and comparisons with examples from Liu Xiang's *Lienü zhuan* and other sources where information can be found about the life of women before and during Ban Zhao's time, indicates that her demands are both more severe and more specific. In order to facilitate a comparative examination of the precepts, I have categorized the kinds of control advocated by Ban Zhao:

1. Control over ideology
2. Control over speech and behaviour
3. Control over divorce and remarriage
4. Control over women's ideology

Control Over Ideology

From the very beginning, Ban Zhao states the position of women in no uncertain terms. The first chapter has the heading: "Lowly and weak", which she says is the position of women and the reason why women are destined to serve others. Not only should a woman be humble and always defer to others, she must "endure insults and swallow smears, and constantly live as in fear".[14] In the second chapter, it is maintained that a husband should learn to control his wife (the verb *yu*, meaning to control horses when driving a carriage, is used), and that a wife should learn to serve her husband. In the third chapter, it is stated that the behaviour of men and women should be different because *yin* (woman) and *yang* (man) have different natures: "*Yang*'s quality is hard and *yin*'s application is soft; men are valued for their strength while women are praised for their weakness." Clarifying this point Ban Zhao cites the aphorism: "Though a boy is born like a wolf, it is still feared that he may grow up to be like a worm, and yet though a girl is born like a mouse, it is still feared that she may grow up to be like a tiger." In short, a girl is not encouraged to be strong and independent, but is trained to be respectful and submissive from birth. However, a contrary view to the implications of these attitudes can be found by examining the theory of *yin* and *yang*, symbolizing man and woman, both in Daoist works and in the Confucian classic the *Yijing*, where *yin* and *yang* clearly represent two equal and mutually complementary opposites. The imbalance of the two is said to lead to problems. From this we might deduce that if *yin* were too weak, it would create an imbalance of the two and would therefore be inauspicious.

---

[14] *Nüjie*, Chapter I, *Hou Han shu*, j. 84, p. 2787. (Hereafter, references to *Nüjie* will only give the chapter number and the page number in *Hou Han shu*.)

It is widely speculated that China went through a phase of matriarchal society before turning into the strongly patriarchal society described and perpetuated by the Confucianists. From the *Lienü zhuan* we learn that neither Qi, the originator of farming in China, nor Xie, Yao's minister in charge of education, had a father;[15] their mothers had miraculously conceived them. Furthermore, they had inherited their respective special abilities, farming and education, from their mothers, Jiangyuan and Jiandi. Though more substantial evidence is yet to be found to prove the existence of such a matriarchial society, Guo Moruo's research on documentary evidence,[16] and the discoveries at the archaeological site at Banpo near Xi'an have made some progress in that direction.[17] Many pre-Qin writers alluded to an antiquity in which people knew their mothers, and not their fathers,[18] and Western scholars have also contributed to this theory. For example, van Gulik has offered five reasons why he thinks that at some stage women were dominant in ancient Chinese society,[19] and Frost has searched for clues from legends and characters to support the thesis of the existence of a Chinese matriarchal society.[20]

Even after the transition to the patriarchal system, the position of women was still not as low as in later dynasties. Men often asked their women for advice, and if a man was in the wrong, his mother, his wife, or even his daughter could remonstrate with him. The *Lienü zhuan* contains ample illustrations of this kind in the first three chapters and many of these stories can be verified in the *Zuo zhuan*. The very first biography in *Lienü zhuan*, that of Ehuang and Nüying, shows that Shun, who later became one of the Sage Emperors exalted by Confucianists, consulted his two wives frequently on matters of importance. To cite a well-known example of a wife admonishing her husband: the wife of the coachman for the Chief Minister of Qi admonished her husband for being arrogant and complacent. She advised him to learn from his master Yan Ying, the Chief Minister. The coachman thanked his wife for correcting him and subsequently changed his ways. When Yan Ying found out, he gave the coachman's wife the

---

[15] According to *Shiji*, Jiangyuan, Qi's mother, was Digu's first consort and Jiandi, Xie's mother, was his second consort. However, this was refuted by one of *Shiji*'s commentators, Jiao Zhou, for the reason that Digu and his alleged offspring were too far apart in time to be father and sons. (See the first paragraph of j. 3 and j. 4 of *Shiji* respectively.) Also in Digu's own biography in the same book (j. 1, p. 14), he was said to have married a daughter of Chen-feng and again a daughter of Juzi. No mention is made of his marriage to Jiangyuan and Jiandi.

[16] Guo Moruo, *Zhongguo gudai shehui yanjiu*, pp. 203-7.

[17] Xi'an Banpo Bowuguan (comp.), *Zhongguo yuanshi shehui*.

[18] *Zhuangzi*, j. 9, p. 19b.

[19] van Gulik, pp. 5-8.

[20] Molly Spitzer Frost, "Chinese Matriarchy: Clues from Legends and Characters" (Ph. D thesis, Georgetown University, 1982).

honorary title *mingfu*. This story is also found in *Shiji* with only one omission—Yan Ying giving the honorary title to the coachman's wife.[21] In this story neither the coachman, a commoner, nor Yan Ying, a high official, thought the wife's behaviour to be out of order.

When Liu Bang, the first emperor of Han, was in the process of building his empire, he constantly sought the advice of his wife. It is said in the *Shiji*, "Empress Lü was strong-willed and persevering by nature, she helped Gaozu (Liu Bang) to acquire the empire; the killing of the great ministers was mostly due to her efforts."[22] (The killing of the great ministers here refers to Liu's eliminating possible competitors for the throne among his own ministers.) The relationship between husband and wife at this time was more like that of two equal partners than that of lord and servant as advocated by Ban Zhao. At a later date Empress Lü was to become the *de facto* ruler of the nation throughout her son's reign, after which she reigned for a further eight years as Dowager Empress until her death. After Empress Lü, seven other empresses reigned as dowagers during the Han dynasty.[23]

In Ban Zhao's own time, Dowager Empress Deng ruled for fifteen years (106-121). Though Dowager Empress Deng is portrayed as the personification of humility in her own biography in the *Hou Han shu*, her scheming and autocratic ways can be seen from other biographies in the same work. She was able to rule because when her husband died, his elder son (by an unknown mother) was not made emperor. In his place the younger son, a sickly infant whom she had adopted, was put on the throne. When the infant emperor died eight months later, at the age of two, she again arranged for another minor be made emperor (Emperor An) so that she could continue to rule as Dowager Empress.[24] Even when Emperor An grew up, she was still unwilling to relinquish power, and eliminated any minister who dared to suggest that power be returned to the emperor.[25] During her rule she entrusted affairs of the state to her brother Deng Zhi, and she enfeoffed her brothers and nephews with large territories.[26] Ministers who did not support her and her clique were ruthlessly suppressed.[27] The Dowager Empress was Ban Zhao's pupil and she made Ban Zhao her most trusted adviser,[28] yet she could hardly be said to have been the exemplification of a self-effacing woman.

---

[21] *Lienü zhuan*, j. 2, Biography 12; *Shiji*, j. 62, p. 2135.

[22] *Shiji*, j. 9, p. 396.

[23] Dowager Empress Wang of Western Han and Dowager Dou, Deng, Yan, Liang, Dou and He of Eastern Han.

[24] *Hou Han shu*, j. 33, p. 1157; j. 55, p. 1803.

[25] *Ibid.*, j. 57, p. 1839.

[26] *Ibid.*, j. 16, pp. 612-17.

[27] *Ibid.*, j. 45, p. 1524; j. 46, p. 1566; j. 60A, p. 1970.

[28] *Ibid.*, j. 84, pp. 2784-5.

Ban Zhao was held in great esteem by both Empress Deng and her husband, Emperor He. She was exalted to a height unmatched in the history of China by any woman (outside royalty). She completed the *Han shu* for her brother, Ban Gu, after his death. Because of the difficulty of the text, not many scholars could fully comprehend it. Ma Rong, who was to become one of the greatest Confucian scholars of the Eastern Han dynasty, studied it under her guidance while prostrated beneath her gallery. She did not exemplify the lowly woman she later advocated so strongly.

Despite her own success in literature, scholarship and politics, she did not encourage other women to follow her footsteps. From her success we must assume that she had received an excellent education in the classics, one that was comparable to that of her brother Gu. Yet, in the second chapter of *Nüjie,* she recommends that women only receive elementary education from the ages of eight to fifteen.[29] In Chapter 4, when she defines the four qualities of a woman, she again set very low standards for them:

> Speaking of a woman's virtue, it is not necessary for her to be brilliant, outstanding or unique. As to a woman's speech, she need not be gifted at debate or be skilled with words. A woman's appearance need not be beautiful, and a woman's work need not be cleverer than others.[30]

She does not encourage them to excel in any area, but counsels them to mediocrity.

Control Over Speech, Behaviour and Movement

On the topic of speech, Ban Zhao advises in Chapter 4: "Choose your words carefully, and utter not vile words. Speak only at the appropriate moment. Avoid offending others (with untactful words or loquacity)." Women are especially discouraged from being argumentative. In the previous section we saw that as a general rule she did not like women to be "gifted in debate and skilled with words". In Chapter 3, she argues that if the husband and wife become too intimate then arguments will occur. When arguments occur, the husband might become angry and beat his wife, thus the love between the couple will be affected and division will ensue. In Chapter 6, women are instructed to obey the mother-in-law regardless of whether the latter is right or wrong. She must not try to argue with the mother-in-law, but should be a shadow and an echo to her.[31]

The *Nüjie* does not state explicitly that women should not go out, perhaps because by this time such a rule had already been established. Ban Zhao goes much further: she spells out a series of interdictions for women:

---

[29] *Nüjie*, Chapter 2, p. 2788.
[30] *Ibid.*, Chapter 4, p. 2789.
[31] *Ibid.*, Chapter 6, p. 2791.

You should watch yourself so that you are always pure and quiet, and love not jesting and laughing.[32]

Concentrate on weaving and spinning, and love not jesting and laughing.[33]

Your ears should not listen to gossip in the street, your eyes should not dart sideway glances; going out you should not put on a seductive appearance, even at home you should not neglect your toilet. You should not gather together with your friends, nor peep out of doors and windows.[34]

If these restrictions were followed to the letter, women would have had to forgo all interests, and enjoy neither relaxation nor entertainment of any kind. They would have been totally isolated from the world outside their own household. In an upper class family where the inner and outer compartments were separated, a woman's world would consist of only the inner compartment of the house. Not only could she not associate with the opposite sex outside her immediate family, but she was discouraged from taking part in gatherings of other women. Thus women in effect became prisoners with a life sentence. But did women really live like that? Evidence from earlier records and records of Ban Zhao's time seems to suggest otherwise.

I have not found references before this period which stipulate that women were not allowed to speak their minds, especially when they were wronged. Many examples of women expressing candid opinions are to be found both in the *Zuo zhuan* and the *Lienü zhuan*: Deng Man, the first consort of King Wu of Chu, gave her husband advice regarding two expeditions, and she told him frankly of his errors and inadequacies;[35] even a commoner such as the girl of the countryside of Chu dared to argue with an official from a neighbouring state when the latter wanted to whip her for accidentally breaking the axle of his carriage;[36] and the mother of Jiangyi, an official of Chu, reprimanded the King for wrongly punishing her son.[37] In fact the whole of Chapter 6 is devoted to such bold and outspoken women.

The interdiction on socializing between men and women did not seem to exist or to be enforced very strictly in pre-Qin times. In the *Shijing*, there are many examples of meetings of girls and boys. *Song* 93 seems to suggest that it was common practice for girls and boys to meet in large numbers outside the city and *Song* 95 describes boys and girls picking flowers and frolicking together on the river banks. From *Song*

---

[32] *Ibid.*, Chapter 1, p. 2787.

[33] *Ibid.*, Chapter 4, p. 2789.

[34] *Ibid.*, Chapter 5, p. 2790.

[35] *Zuo zhuan*, Duke of Huan 13th year; *Lienü zhuan*, j. 3, Biography 2.

[36] *Lienü zhuan*, j. 6, Biography 5.

[37] *Ibid.*, j. 6, Biography 2.

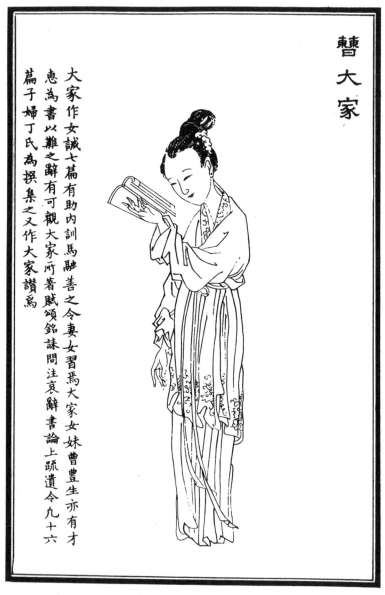

曹大家

大家作女誡七篇有助内訓焉融善之令妻女習焉大家女妹曹豐生亦有才

惠為書以難之辭有可觀大家所著賦頌銘誄問注哀辭書論上疏遺令九十六

篇子婦丁氏為撰集之又作大家讚焉

A Qing Dynasty artist's portrait of Ban Zhao (i.e., Cao *dagu*). From *Wanxiaotang hua zhuan*.

76 we learn that men sometimes scaled walls to meet their lovers at night. The *Shijing* was said to have been compiled by Confucius, yet poems like these have survived without apparent censorship by the Great Sage. Possibly the moral climate of the period preceding him was comparatively liberal, and Confucius himself had a more tolerant attitude toward men and women meeting socially than is generally believed. In the *Lunyu* it is recorded that he visited the consort of Duke Ling of Wei, Nanzi, who was famous for both her beauty and her loose morals. Though Confucius denied having any improper motives, he did not deny the fact that the meeting actually took place.[38]

In other works of the same period we can also find examples which suggest that women had more freedom of movement. Women of ordinary families were responsible for sharing the farmwork. Ehuang and Nüying, though daughters of King Yao, served Shun in the fields.[39] Admittedly, Shun existed in such an early age that information concerning him and his two wives is closer to legend than historical fact. However, Liu Xiang obviously did not consider this act improper, otherwise he would not have included it in the biography of these two exemplary women. Empress Lü also worked in the fields before Liu Bang rose against the Qin emperor.[40] Sericulture was a very important part of a woman's work, and it was necessary for women to go out to pick mulberry leaves in order to feed the silkworms. To save on the labour of carrying water to the house, women often washed clothes by the side of rivers or creeks. Such chores took women outside their homes and brought them into contact with strangers. We read of Empress Lü being approached by an old man for a drink of water.[41] There are cases of women who meet men while they are picking mulberry leaves: in *Lienü zhuan*,[42] as well as in an anonymous folk song among the *yuefu* dated around the Han dynasty.[43] We also find in *Lienü zhuan* the example in which Confucius sent Zigong to talk to a girl washing at Egu outside the city.[44] Upper class women were probably more restricted in their movements, yet they were not entirely confined to the palaces. In the *Lienü zhuan* we read that wives often accompanied their husbands on pleasure trips. Mengji, the first consort of Duke Xiao of Qi, accompanied her husband on a trip to Langye, while King Zhao of Chu took two of his concubines with him when

---

[38] *Lunyu*, j. 6, p. 5b.

[39] *Lienü zhuan*, j. 1, Biography 1.

[40] *Shiji*, j. 8, p. 346.

[41] *Ibid.*

[42] *Lienü zhuan*, j. 6, Biography 6.

[43] "Moshang sang", in *Han-Wei yuefu feng jian,* published as *Gushi jishi deng sizhong*, j. 1, p. 10.

[44] *Lienü zhuan*, j. 6, Biography 6.

he made a pleasure trip;[45] on a later occasion the same concubines again accompanied him on an expedition to aid the State of Chen.

One of the most vivid descriptions of men and women socializing freely comes from Chunyu Kun's biography in the *Shiji*:

> But if there is a feast of local residents (*lüli zhi hui*) in which men and women are mixed in the seating, people take turns to drink leisurely while others gather a few friends together to gamble in *liubo* and *touhu*. On such occasions, holding hands is not punishable nor is staring prohibited.
>
> Here and there one can see earrings and hairpins which have fallen off and been left behind. In my heart I love such occasions, hence I can drink eight piculs and only get twenty to thirty per cent drunk. At sunset when the drinkers have thinned out, we pool our bottles and sit around more closely together, a man and a woman would sit on the same seat, his shoes mixed up with hers. The cups and plates are left in disarray, while the candles in the hall go out, and the hostess asks me to stay behind after seeing all her guests off. The lapel of her silk blouse has come unfastened so that I can faintly smell her body fragrance. At this moment, my heart is at its happiest and I can drink ten piculs.[46]

Chunyu Kun was a jester at the court of Duke Wei of Qi in the Warring States Period. The speech which is partially quoted above is meant to be in jest, so the condition described may be exaggerated. However, even after making the utmost allowance for this, the passage suggests a freer society than Ban Zhao's prescription as far as association between men and women is concerned.

Control Over Divorce and Remarriage

Following books on rites and propriety compiled in the Han dynasty, Ban Zhao stressed the rule that a man can remarry while a woman may never do so. In Chapter 5 of *Nüjie* she gives the following reason:

> According to the books on propriety, there is justification for men to remarry, but there is no text upon which the remarriage of women can be based. Hence we say, the husband is like heaven; there is no way we can escape from heaven, similarly, women cannot leave their husbands.

Since under no circumstance can a woman leave her husband, then no matter what kind of a man he turns out to be, she must live with him and obey him. Her whole future depends on him, therefore it is imperative that she please him. Ban Zhao goes on in the same chapter to quote the *Nü xian*:

> If you please one man, your whole life is made; if you lose the pleasure of one man, your whole life is finished.

---

[45] *Lienü zhuan*, j. 4, Biography 6 and j. 5, Biography 4, respectively.
[46] *Shiji*, j. 126, p. 3199.

Since a woman has to do anything to please her husband, Ban Zhao argues, it follows that she must be willing to do anything to please the husband's parents and brothers and sisters. Consequently she has to submit her own will to that of the whole family.

Scholars have already observed that remarriage of widows was not an uncommon phenomenon in ancient China. Based on records of the pre-Qin period, Liu Dehan concludes that during Eastern Zhou, apart from a few women who preferred not to, the majority of widows did remarry. In fact, often when the women themselves did not wish to remarry, their families or the authorities would coerce them into remarriage.[47] Liu also points out that not only could widows remarry but that women who had been divorced by their husbands also had the same right. Jack Dull collated various cases of women remarrying in the Han dynasty, and concludes that for both men and women, it was customary for them to remarry if their spouses had died or if they had been divorced.[48] Liu Xiang's *Lienü zhuan* is the first work we know of that has devoted a great deal of attention to the concept of chastity. Chaste women occupy two out of the seven chapters of his book. (The eighth chapter was a supplement appended to his work at a later time.) Yet O'Hara has found two cases in the *Lienü zhuan* in which a wife left, and another threatened to leave, her husband.[49] Dull also cites cases in the Han dynasty in which women left their husbands, as well as one case in which the wife's family initiated a divorce.[50] It seems that it was not particularly unusual for women to leave their husbands even though an official divorce had not been effected.

In view of the foregoing comparisons, it is clear that the standards recommended by Ban Zhao are far more stringent than those generally in practice prior to and during the Han dynasty. An explanation for this may be found by an investigation of the trend of Han thought and its influence on social attitudes in Eastern Han.

From "Rulin zhuan", the chapter on Confucian scholarship in all three of the official histories covering the Han dynasty, i.e. *Shiji, Han shu* and *Hou Han shu*, we can see that in the beginning of Western Han, Daoist influence was prominent. Despite the fact that in the reign of Emperor Wu Confucianism was held as orthodox, and the state ceased to recognize all other schools of thought, the succeeding monarchs again turned to Daoism. However, after the establishment of the Eastern Han dynasty, all the emperors from Emperor Guangwu to Emperor He held Confucianism in high esteem and took a personal interest in its teaching and propagation. At the same time, a conservative trend started to gradually grow in reaction to the fairly

---

[47] Liu Dehan, *Dong Zhou funü shenghuo*, pp. 63-64.

[48] Jack Dull, *op. cit.,* pp. 64-7.

[49] Albert Richard O'Hara, *The Position of Women in Early China According to the Lieh Nü Chuan, "The Biographies of Chinese Women"*, p. 277.

[50] Dull, *op. cit.,* pp. 61-2.

relaxed social control in Western Han, a fact which Eastern Han scholars saw as the cause of moral degeneration from the high standards of the ancients. The palace women of the Western Han emperors are renowned for their lowly origins and low moral calibre. Liu Xiang is said to have compiled his *Lienü zhuan* because:

> He saw that the customs of the time were getting more extravagant and immoral. (Empress) Zhao (Feiyan) and (Empress) Wei (Zifu) rose from lowly and unworthy families and exceeded the bounds of propriety. Xiang was of the opinion that the teaching of the ruler should come from within his family and extend outwards, beginning from those closest to him. So he selected from the *Songs* and the *Documents* wise consorts and chaste women who had made a country prosper or a family famous, as well as those who were pernicious and depraved, and had caused the disorder or the ruin of a country or a family. He then organized their lives into the *Lienü zhuan* in eight volumes so as to admonish the emperor.[51]

The Ban family had a lot in common with the Liu family. Both produced great scholars who at some stage of their career were appointed to the Imperial Library as editors. In fact, Ban Zhao's great uncle Ban You had worked with Liu Xiang in the Imperial Library.[52] In both families, the father had started an important writing project which was completed by his son. Most important of all, both were Confucian in their basic philosophy. Dull notes that many Han scholars felt that the pre-Qin rites had been lost during the Qin dynasty and the ensuing upheavals, and that while the Han dynasty had muddled through thus far without proper rites, there was a need to formulate a set of comprehensive rites. He goes on to list the efforts made by scholars in Eastern Han, amongst them Ban Zhao and her brother Gu, to address this problem.[53] His view that Ban Zhao's *Nüjie* is not a description of common practice but rather a list of prescriptive norms for the conduct of a woman's life is definitely closer to the truth.

Ban Zhao's precepts are detailed and practical, and cover virtually every aspect of a woman's life; the controls imposed were therefore equally comprehensive. Like other Confucian thinkers of her time, Ban Zhao wanted to restrain people's behaviour with propriety. In this may lie Ban Zhao's real motive for writing the *Nüjie*. Her professed motive—that she wrote it for the guidance of "my girls"—may have been nothing but a pretext. I am basing this hypothesis on two arguments. Firstly, as pointed out above, she was fifty-four or more when she wrote *Nüjie*. Her biography tells us that she was married at the age of fourteen and that she was widowed at a young age. From the combination of these factors it is reasonable to assume that at the time she wrote the work her children would have been in the age group of thirty to forty, and therefore well past the marrying age. It is, of

---

[51] *Han shu*, j. 36, p. 1957.
[52] *Ibid*, j. 100A, p. 4202.
[53] Dull, *op. cit.*, pp. 36-8.

course, possible that "my girls" refers to her granddaughters, but this does not seem likely from the context. Secondly, at this stage of her life, Ban Zhao was a well respected public figure who could count even the Dowager Empress among her pupils. She could not have written *Nüjie* without at least being aware of the influence it might have on the education of girls in general. Therefore I believe she wrote it with the intention of establishing a standard for women of all ages. It was her contribution to the Han Confucian movement which aimed at bringing about a more orderly society based on Confucian propriety. However, the mould she created was so constraining that the individual who tried to conform risked suffocation. The woman would end up with no personality of her own, as she would not be able to think her own thoughts, speak her own mind or do as she chose. All her life she would be trying to please her husband, his parents and brothers and sisters. If, in the unfortunate event that she failed to do so, the consequences would be absolutely tragic, because that would mean the end of her happiness for the rest of her life.

According to her biography, the reaction to *Nüjie* in Ban Zhao's own lifetime was mixed. Her own sister-in-law was critical and wrote a letter to debate her views. On the other hand, her pupil Ma Rong thought it was good and asked his wife and daughters to study it. The biographies of Ma Rong's two daughters are to be found in the same chapter as Ban Zhao's biography in *Hou Han shu.* They do not appear to have been brought up according to Ban Zhao's precepts. Lun, the elder, is portrayed as gifted in debating. On two occasions she had argued with her husband, something against which Ban Zhao had specifically remonstrated. The younger daughter, Zhi, is said to have composed a poetic essay entitled "Shenqing fu" (Poetic essay to express one's feelings), so she must have received more than the elementary education recommended by Ban Zhao.

Following Ban Zhao's era, China fell into a long period of relaxed morals when comparatively little attention was given to her *Nüjie.* It was not until Neo-Confucianism had made its mark on Chinese thought that Emperor Shen of the Ming dynasty ordered his minister Wang Xiang to prepare notes for the *Nüjie* and published it together with Empress Xu's *Neixun* in 1580. Later, together with two more works, *Nü Lunyu* by Song Ruozhao (Tang dynasty) and Madam Liu's *Nüfan jielu* (Ming dynasty), they were republished as the *Four Books for Women.* From then onward, Ban Zhao's work gained wide circulation, for just as every literate man started his education with the *Four Books*, every literate woman began hers with the *Four Books for Women.* This situation continued until modern education modelled on the West supplanted traditional education. Hence Ban Zhao's influence on the life of women from late-Ming to at least the fall of Qing cannot be over-emphasized. More and more women were expected to conform to the idealistic pattern delineated by Ban Zhao and others. As a result, lifelong celibacy of young widows and persecution of remarried women robbed many women of a happy domestic life. Worse still, young girls were made to marry a rooster when their betrothed died and widows were even encouraged to commit suicide on the death of their husbands. Ban Zhao did not intend, nor could she foresee, that centuries later her precepts would start a trend which would develop and snowball into the "man-eating rites and teachings" against which the May Fourth generation would vehemently rebel.

Xie Daoyun: The Style of a Woman *Mingshi*

Of the outstanding women throughout Chinese history known to us, most are writers. The personality and outlook reflected in most of their works are typically "feminine" in the narrow sense of the word. Generally speaking, their style is fresh and intimate, while the content usually falls into the categories of love, loneliness, natural beauty and details relating to life in the confinement of the women's quarters. Very few departures were made from these so called "feminine" themes.

The two exceptions are Ban Zhao of Eastern Han and Xie Daoyun of Eastern Jin. Ban Zhao not only completed her brother Ban Gu's unfinished history of the Han dynasty, *Han shu*, but also wrote a textbook for the instruction of girls, as well as many literary works covering a variety of subjects and reflecting a much wider outlook than the traditionally feminine one. Although not many of Xie Daoyun's works are extant, it is clear that her style, both personal and literary, as reflected by her biography in the official history and other related works, broke away from the feminine tradition. Her thinking extended beyond the confinement of her own domestic world; her intellectual outlook equalled in scope and depth that of the contemporary male scholars, and her debating talent was comparable or superior to that of the men of her time. What is more unusual is that in her judgement and courage she frequently surpassed men of her time by a long way. Hence, if we try to categorize her according to the terminology of her time, she could without reservation be described as a woman *mingshi*.

Mingshi, literally, means "famous scholar", but its connotation has changed with the times. When it first appeared in common use in the Eastern Han dynasty, it referred to scholars who had won fame through their integrity and virtue. However, after the Wei-Jin period, the "famous scholar" developed into an archetype. No definition of this term can be found, but from a sarcastic comment made by an Eastern Jin scholar a notion as to what it typified can be constructed: "To be a 'famous scholar' one does not need to have talent; one only has to have nothing to do most of the time, drink heartily and recite the *Lisao* by heart. Thereby one can be called a 'famous scholar'".

Although these words were spoken in jest, the prerequisites of a "famous scholar" are indeed all contained therein. First of all, it stipulates that the "famous scholar" must "have nothing to do most of the time" which means he must be born into an élite family so as to free him from working for a living. Secondly, the "famous scholar" must "drink heartily", as drinking was a symbol of untrammelled behaviour and a concrete expression of anti-ritualistic thinking. Among the "Seven Worthies of the Bamboo Grove", whose lifestyle was seen to challenge the Confucian tradition and to advocate a Neo-Daoist standard of behaviour, Liu Ling and Ruan Ji were continually drunk but were portrayed in a favourable light because of it. Thirdly, to recite the

Lisao by heart implies that a famous scholar must be well versed in literature. This can be taken further to mean that he must be well versed in literature and philosophy and be a talented debater. *Lisao* expresses the poet's dissatisfaction with, and his aspiration to transcend, reality. Hence it was also in line with the popular philosophical trend of the time. In short, a "famous scholar" must be born into an élite family, inclined towards the Daoist belief in the untrammelled and reclusive way of life, and actually living according to this belief, as well as being well versed in literature and philosophy.

These, then, are the prerequisites of a "famous scholar". It was not at all an easy thing for a woman to satisfy these prerequisites in traditional China. To be born into an élite family was something decided by pure chance, the odds of which is one in thousands. To be well versed in literature and philosophy was hard enough, but to be able to utilize the knowledge and perception in the art of *qingtan*, philosophical discourse and debate, even for men would require a considerable amount of talent and hard work. Moreover, in a society in which women were not encouraged to excel in learning, those who reached such a level might not have the courage to show it and to be recognized for it. Only under certain very specific social conditions could a woman "famous scholar" like Xie Daoyun emerge.

The Wei-Jin period was a transitional period in Chinese history. Politically, after the great upheaval at the end of Eastern Han and the incessant incursions of minority races from the borders, the great empire disintegrated and for centuries stability could not be re-established. Following the loss of political stability, people's faith in Confucianism, the principal guiding philosophy of Han, was also shaken. All the social institutions—both written and unwritten— related to Confucianism and were no longer strictly upheld by the people. Daoism, which had always had a special attraction for intellectuals of turbulent times, arose to fill the vacuum thus created. This trend was established from the time when Wang Bi (226-251) and He Yan (190-249) advocated *xuanxue* (metaphysical study) and *qingtan* (philosophical discourse), and continued to be popular for the next few centuries. It was not until the Tang dynasty that the pendulum of Chinese thought swung back towards Confucianism. *Xuanxue* was a metaphysical school which fused the philosophies of the Confucian classic *Yijing* and the Daoist philosophy of Laozi and Zhuangzi. After Eastern Jin, Buddhist thought was added to the hybrid. Yet it often adopted the form and technique of *Mingjia*, the Dialecticians. Apart from writing theoretical treatises, adepts often gathered together for discussions and debate. Such gatherings were known as *qingtan*, philosophical discourse. In the Six Dynasties period, philosophical discourse was not only of academic significance, it also had a practical social value, as it was a means by which scholars could achieve fame and fortune. If a scholar performed outstandingly in a philosophical discourse, he could become a "famous scholar" overnight. The political leaders of the time were immersed in the practice of philosophical discourse, and also frequently promoted younger scholars gifted in the art.[1] Hence, philosophical discourse became a stepping stone for officialdom and everyone, regardless of his current social position, practised it. Moreover, even people who had no interest in becoming officials practised it, as once they won acclaim, their social position would be higher than the political leaders by virtue of their pure and lofty aspirations in rejecting worldly honour and gain.

The flourishing of Daoist thought was often the catalyst for the rise of individualism, and symptomatic of times when social constraints were weak. We have no clear documentary evidence of the Daoist view towards women, although from such ideas as "return to nature" and "equality of all things" it is possible to speculate that there was less inclination to advocate the use of artificial moral constraints on women. Hence, in the Wei-Jin period, women had comparatively more freedom to develop their personality and talent. Some of them went into the political and economic arenas: for example, Empress Jia and Wang Dao's concubine (née Lei) both interfered in the affairs of the state,[2] and Wang Yan's wife (née Guo) and Wang Rong's wife (name unknown) were notorious for amassing great fortunes.[3] In the academic, literary and artistic fields, there were Xie Daoyun, Lady Wei (teacher of the great calligrapher Wang Xizhi), Zuo Fen and Bao Linghui who were famous women writers of both poetry and prose.[4]

Another trend of this period also provided a favourable milieu for some women to develop their own interests. This was the emergence of an élitist clan system. In this social system, certain clans enjoyed special prestige and privileges. All members of these clans enjoyed elevated social positions by birth. They had priority access to official positions and socially were sought out as friends and marriage partners. After a few generations, they believed that they were actually superior to others. This superiority complex was common among the male members of these clans, and was shared by the females members. To these women with their special status, came privileges not possessed by ordinary women, such as learning to read, studying philosophy, teaching, writing, running the country behind the scenes and engaging in economic activities. Because of faith in their own superiority, these women found it difficult to play the role of the submissive and contented wife, especially when the position of the husband's clan or the talent of the husband could not measure up to her own.

---

[1] *Shishuo xinyu jiaojian*, V, 18 tells a story in which a young man gained an appointment by uttering three words which pleased a powerful man.

[2] *Jin shu*, j. 31, pp. 963-6; *Shishuo xinyu jiaojian*, XXXV, 7.

[3] *Shishuo xinyu jiaojian*, XXIX, 3; *Jin shu*, j. 43, p. 1237.

[4] For their lives and work, see Xie Wuliang, *Zhongguo funü wenxueshi*, Section IIB: Wei-Jin Nan-bei-chao.

Moreover, after the tremendous upheaval at the end of Western Jin, there were many movements in the population. Many families were split. Sometimes the husband fled to the South while the wife stayed behind in the North; sometimes one of them was made prisoner and taken behind enemy lines, and so on. Under such circumstances, women were forced to try to survive by their own wits, hence the number of women living independently and remarrying gradually grew. The rules of propriety used in a normal society were by necessity temporarily readjusted or disregarded in view of the chaotic times. Under such circumstances, the constraints placed on a woman's activities naturally had to be relaxed.

Xie Daoyun was born in Eastern Jin, a period which followed the upheaval mentioned above. She was also a member of one of the two most prestigious clans, Wang and Xie, and as such she was able to enjoy the relatively relaxed constraints of the time on women and also to make use of the extra freedom to which she was entitled as a member of the élite. Under such favourable conditions she was able to become an important link in the long chain of outstanding women in China.

Xie Daoyun came from the Xie clan of Yangxia in the state of Chen (modern Henan). Her great, great grandfather Zan was already an official; his highest position was Captain of Squires in the Agriculture Office, probably a middle to high level military officer.[5] Her great grandfather Xie Heng was an Erudite of the State Academy at the end of the Taikang reign (280-290), and was later promoted to Chancellor. In other words, he was an important intellectual towards the end of Western Jin. From the memorials which he left behind, we know that he helped the court to solve some problems concerning ritual and propriety using arguments based on the Confucian classics.[6] Moreover, from *Zhongxing shu*, quoted in the commentary of *Shishuo xinyu*, we learn that he had attained the position of Junior Tutor to the Heir Apparent, a position of high prestige and few duties.[7]

Daoyun's great uncle Xie Kun was the first "famous scholar" of the Xie clan. He was one of the group of scholars known as the *Ba Da*, "The Eight Untrammelled Ones", who became well known at the end of Western Jin for their unconventional behaviour. This group comprised some of the outstanding members of the élite clans and their friends; in behaviour, they emulated the bizarre and uninhibited style of Ruan Ji.[8] In the era when *xuanxue* was the prevailing philosophy of the time, unconventional behaviour was viewed as a sign of lofty

---

[5] *Jin shu*, j. 49, p. 1377.

[6] Yan Kejun, *Quan Jin wen*, j. 83, pp. 1a & b.

[7] *Shishuo xinyu jiaojian*, I, 33.

[8] Ruan Ji (210-263) was a member of a group later known as the "Seven Worthies of the Bamboo Grove", famous for their achievements in philosophy and literature as well as unconventional behaviour.

thinking and consequently a desirable trait in a scholar. For that reason Xie Kun was taken by Sima Yue, Prince of Donghai, into his circle of advisers and assistants. During Eastern Jin he was also admired by Wang Dun and became Wang's subordinate. At the time Wang Dun and his cousin Wang Dao controlled respectively military and political power of the Eastern Jin regime. Their influence almost exceeded that of the court which had only just been established south of the Yangtze River after the fall of the Northern capital Chang'an (modern Xi'an). Consequently, Wang Dun began to harbour thoughts of usurpation. This put Xie Kun in an awkward situation: on the one hand, he was reluctant to help Wang Dun in his plans of usurpation, on the other, his life and that of his family were in the hands of the irascible General. Under such precarious circumstances, most people were afraid to speak out against Wang; only Xie Kun admonished Wang Dun repeatedly, at the risk of his own life. Although Wang Dun did not change his mind, neither did he kill Xie, owing to the latter's great reputation in the nation. Xie Kun's ability to disregard his own future and safety in the face of difficulty and danger made him a model for the "famous scholars" of the Xie clan. Among those who proved to have inherited his ability to keep his wits and principles in a crisis were his son Xie Shang, his nephew Xie An, his grand niece Xie Daoyun, and his grand nephews Xie Xuan and Xie Yan.

Because of Xie Kun's unflinching loyalty, after his death his descendants were amply rewarded with imperial favours. Xie Shang, his son, was like his father in his disregard for formalities. Wang Dao, the prime minister of the time, and his patron, once asked him to do the Mina Bird Dance. Without the slightest hesitation he started to dance in full official attire. The historian uses this story to illustrate the unaffected nature of his character. Xie Shang inherited his father's position and title and went on to attain even higher positions. He was Governor of Yuzhou in charge of the military affairs of four states, a position which carried both prestige and real power at the provincial level, followed by Vice-Director of the Imperial Secretariat, a position at court of the first order which embodied both power and prestige in the central government. Having no heir of his own, after his death his positions were passed on to his cousin Xie Yi, Xie Daoyun's father, while his title was inherited by Yi's son Kang who was appointed his heir posthumously.

Xie Daoyun's grandfather Xie Pou was Xie Kun's brother. Though he was not as well known as Xie Kun, he also attained a high official position as the Minister of Personnel. Xie Pou had six sons, the eldest being Xie Yi. The others were: Xie Ju, Xie An, Xie Wan, Xie Shi and Xie Tie. Xie Ju died early in his life.

Xie Yi, Daoyun's father, was not an outstanding scholar. According to *Shishuo xinyu,* in his early years when he was a magistrate, he used torture on an elderly prisoner and was admonished by his younger

29

brother Xie An.[9] Later, because of his friendship with Huan Wen, he went to Jingzhou as Military Commander when Huan was appointed Governor of Jingzhou. The only outstanding quality we know of him is that he did not change his casual manners with Huan Wen after Huan had become a powerful warlord and his superior. This disregard for social distinction and worldly values is considered the true colour of a "famous scholar". Not long afterwards, he succeeded Xie Shang's positions and became an important political and military figure. But before long he died and his positions went to his younger brother Xie Wan.

Xie An and Xie Wan enjoyed equal fame in their youth; they were both leaders of the intellectual world of Eastern Jin. Xie Wan wrote *Baxian lun* (Treatise on the Eight Worthies), a re-evaluation of eight historical figures of the past using the reclusive philosophy which was popular at the time. The Xie brothers counted as their friends some of the most distinguished philosophers and adepts of philosophical discourse, such as the Buddhist monk Daolin, the calligrapher Wang Xizhi, as well as Xu Xun and Yin Hao. Judging from the comments made about them by their contemporaries which appear in *Shishuo xinyu,* the brothers were generally admired by their peers. Later, Xie Wan was demoted for failure to control his army and died of humiliation and grief.

From the beginning, Xie An considered himself a recluse. Before the age of forty he is said to have "nurtured his aspiration [to become a recluse] by the sea in the company of children and those who shared his interest".[10] He lived away from the capital Jiankang (modern Nanjing) in the county of Kuaiji (present day Shangyu district, Zhejiang province). He already enjoyed a great reputation and was repeatedly summoned by the Court, but he persistently declined to accept any official position until the age of forty. Due to his outstanding ability, once he had accepted an official position he rose quickly to an office equivalent to that of prime minister. It was a period in which the Eastern Jin court was threatened from all sides. Externally it was faced with the danger of an invasion by Fu Jian of the Di minority which had occupied North China. Internally it was troubled by the possibility of usurpation by the powerful warlord Huan Wen. Xie An guided the government through troubled waters with pacifying policies and showed strength when it was needed. He led the loyalists in resisting Huan Wen's moves towards seizing the throne. Once Huan asked Xie An and Wang Tanzhi to attend a meeting at a hall in which he hid heavily armed strong men, intending to kill them if talks did not go in his favour. Xie An pretended that nothing was wrong and calmly sang in his old Chang'an style. This literally disarmed Huan who was thus

---

[9] *Shishuo xinyu jiaojian,* I, 33.
[10] Tang Qiu, *Jin yangqiu jiben,* TSCC, no. 3805, p. 69.

reassured that it was still possible to diffuse the confrontation between the two camps. When Huan fell sick and wanted to accelerate the process of usurpation by asking the court to bestow on him the "Nine Gifts", symbol of extraordinary favour, Xie estimated correctly that Huan did not have long to live and used delaying tactics. Huan died soon afterwards without achieving his life-long goal.

As to Fu Jian's invasion, he emulated the "empty city" tactic of Zhuge Liang by appearing completely confident in the strength of the Jin army, thereby allaying the panic in the capital. Meanwhile, he sent his younger brother Xie Shi, his nephew Xie Xuan (Daoyun's brother) and his son Xie Yan to fight Fu Jian. They won a resounding victory at the Fei River against overwhelming odds and became national heroes overnight. This battle, known as The Battle of Fei River, not only earned tremendous fame and merit for the Xie clan, but also stopped the southward movement of the non-Han peoples from the North, at least for the time being, hence prolonging the life of the southern regimes for a few hundred years more. For this reason, the Xie clan was highly regarded throughout the Southern Dynasties and was firmly established as one of the two most prestigious clans of that period. In short, the elevated position of the Xie clan was begun by Xie Heng and Xie Kun and was developed to its highest level by Xie An.

Daoyun's father Yi had seven children, although in his biography in *Jin shu* only three are mentioned: Xie Quan,[11] Xie Jing and Xie Xuan. Xie Shang's biography states that when Shang died, his cousin Yi's son Kang inherited his title.[12] So we know that Xie Yi had four sons, one of whom was adopted posthumously by Xie Shang. In Xie Xuan's biography he is quoted as saying that he had seven siblings (*tongsheng qi ren*).[13] It could easily follow that the other three were daughters, so Daoyun should have had two sisters. However, in the next sentence he said that all of them died and he was the only one left. We know for sure that Daoyun survived Xuan (who died in 388), and died after the year 399 (see below), hence the seven he referred to must all have been male siblings, three of them not having lived long enough to be mentioned in Xie Yi's biography. Among Daoyun's brothers, Xie Kang was adopted posthumously by Xie Shang and died early. Xie Quan became well known early in his life and attained the position of Prefect of Yixing, while Jie Ying reached the position of Chamberlain

---

[11] His original name was Yuan, but Tang historians used Quan to avoid the taboo on the word "yuan".

[12] *Jin shu*, j. 79, p. 2072.

[13] *Ibid.*, p. 2085.

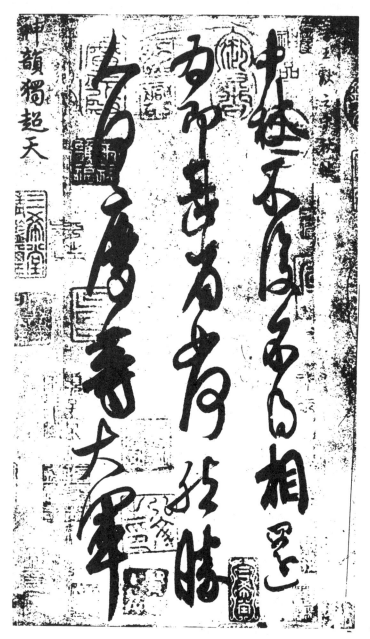

Calligraphy of Wang Xianzhi, Xie Daoyun's brother-in-law to whom Xie once offered her assistance to win a debate.

for Ceremonials. Judging from the powerful position occupied by the Xie clan, it would seem that neither of these two were of particular significance. Their biographies, consisting of only a few sentences, had little to say about them.

Only about Xie Xuan do we know a great deal. Among the members of the younger generation of the Xie clan, Xie Xuan and his sister Daoyun won the commendation of their uncle Xie An from childhood. When he grew up, he was appointed as an aide to his father's old friend and superior Huan Wen and was held in high esteem by the latter. During that time, Fu Jian's regime grew stronger by the day. After unifying the whole of North China, he was waiting for the right moment to take Eastern Jin into his possession. For that reason, the Eastern Jin court was anxious to find a good military leader to defend its northern border. Xie An was in charge of the affairs of the state at the time. Risking the possibility of being accused of nepotism, he recommended his nephew, Xie Xuan, for this vital task. Fortunately for him, Xie Xuan gained one victory after another and at the Fei River, leading the vanguard, he won the decisive battle. After this famous battle, Xie An suggested to the court that Eastern Jin should take the initiative and began an expedition into North China. With Xie Xuan at the head of the army, they recovered many places in present Shandong, Henan and Hebei. Unfortunately, Xie An died in 385, and soon afterwards Xie Xuan fell ill and asked to be relieved of duty. The court did not grant him leave for a long time. He was seriously ill when he was finally relieved of his military duties and given a civilian position in his home county Kuaiji. He died soon afterwards in 388, at the early age of forty-six, only three years after Xie An's death. Though nothing explicit is said in the official history about this, his death following so soon after his uncle's could have been caused by Sima Daozi's refusal to relieve him of his position as the defender of the border even when he was very ill.

Daozi, Prince of Kuaiji and Emperor Xiaowu's brother, succeeded Xie An at the helm of the nation. Before his death, Xie An had always tried to avoid confrontation and competition with Daozi because he knew that, due to its prestige, the Xie clan aroused jealousy in many quarters.[14] Hence after Xie An's death, Daozi could not be expected to be co-operative with the northern expedition; on the contrary, he tried to hold it back. Consequently, though the Eastern Jin regime won a resounding victory at the Fei River, the absence of a capable leader after the deaths of Xie An and Xie Xuan, coupled with the dissipated life of the imperial house, soon led to its deterioration and ultimate demise.

Although Xie Xuan had been commended by his uncle Xie An for being quick-witted and astute, as well as being described as "capable of

---

[14] *Ibid.*, j. 79, p. 2079.

philosophical discourse and good at logic"[15] by his contemporaries, he was not a typical "famous scholar". His achievements were on the battlefields. He did not display special interest in the political or intellectual realm.

In summary, Xie Daoyun's clan was first known for its tradition of Confucian studies. Perhaps due to the trend of the time, the members of the Xie clan beginning with Xie Kun turned to Daoist thinking. Their speech, behaviour and world view reflected strong Daoist tendencies. On the political and military side they produced Xie Kun, Xie Shang, Xie An and Xie Xuan; in philosophy and literature, they produced Xie An and Xie Wan. Their prestige became so high in the Southern Dynasties that they could bestow legitimacy on any regime by throwing their weight behind it. As each dynasty was proclaimed, the new ruler made sure that a representative from each of the two leading clans, the Wangs and the Xies, were at hand to present him with the imperial seal and the ribbon, to render legitimacy to his regime. This fact alone demonstrates to us the special position the Xie clan occupied during that period.

The first-hand sources containing information on Xie Daoyun's life and work are her biography in the *Jin shu*'s chapter on eminent women (j. 96), *Shishuo xinyu, Quan Jin wen* and *Quan Jin shi*. Among the biographies in *Jin shu*'s chapter on eminent women, Daoyun's is the longest one. This could be construed to mean that in the eyes of the Tang historians who compiled the *Jin shu*, she was deemed the most important. There are four entries in *Shishuo xinyu* about Xie Daoyun. The commentary of a fifth also contains her dialogue with an important figure of this period. *Quan Jin wen* contains a fragment of a composition entitled "In Praise of the *Lunyu*" culled from *Yiwen leiju*. *Quan Jin shi* contains fragments of three poems from the same source.

Her official biography in *Jin shu* does not mention her birth and death dates and we can only obtain some approximations by the use of circumstantial evidence. We know that she was Xie Xuan's elder sister, so we know that the year of her birth must be earlier than his in 343. Her biography stated that she was intelligent and perceptive; in addition, she was quick-witted and a talented debater. Two illustrations were given:

> Her uncle once asked, "Which are the best lines in the *Shijing*?"
> Daoyun answered,
>   "I, Jifu, have composed this ode,
>   May it be like a light breeze,
>   Soothing Zhong Shanfu's mind,
>   That is constantly burdened with worries."[16]

---

[15] *Shishuo xinyu jiaojian*, IV, 41.

[16] *Maoshi zhengyi*, j. 18C, p. 10b.

An said that she possessed the profound understanding of a *ya* poet.[17]
Another time, they had a family gathering. In a few moments, a sudden
flurry of snow fell.

> An said, "What can this be likened to?"
> An's elder brother's son Lang said,
>   "It's almost like
>   Scattering salt in the sky."
> Daoyun said,
>   "Not as good as willow catkins borne on the wind."
> An was greatly pleased.[18]

From these two anecdotes we can speculate on the education and
training she received in her youth. The first anecdote suggests that she
had not only studied the *Shijing* but had a deep appreciation of its
aesthetic value. The second anecdote suggests that not only did she
write prose and poetry, she was so skilled in such activities that she
could effortlessly play literary games with the other members of the
family. Hence there is no doubt that she had received a thorough
education, comparable to all her brothers and male cousins.

Since the Xie clan had a long history in Confucian studies, as
suggested by her great grandfather's life described above, Daoyun must
have been familiar with all the Confucian classics. At the same time,
as many of her elders had Daoist tendencies in their thinking, she must
also have at least dabbled in Daoist works. These assumptions can be
confirmed by the fragments of her work available to us now and in the
records of her philosophical discourses found in *Shishuo xinyu*.
Furthermore, we can also infer that she would frequently have had
discussions and debates with her uncle, brothers and cousins on
academic topics, and that they would have read and criticized each
other's literary works. This can also be confirmed by the fact that she
left two *juan* of works, as recorded by the bibliographical chapter of
Sui shu.[19]

Among all the members of the Xie family, the one having the most
profound influence on Daoyun was her uncle, Xie An. His influence on
her possibly exceeded that of her own father. This was due to the fact
that her father, Xie Yi, had always been away from home in various
official positions, while Xie An did not accept any appointments before
the age of forty, and hence had ample time to spend with the younger
generation. As mentioned earlier, he was said to have "nurtured his
aspiration by the sea in the company of children and those who shared
his interest". From the several anecdotes in the *Shishuo xinyu* in
which his conversation with various members of the younger
generation are described, we note that these children not only included

---

[17] *Ya* is the section of the *Shijing* from which this quotation comes.

[18] *Jin shu*, j. 96, p. 2516.

[19] *Sui shu*, j. 35, p. 1070.

his own but those of his brothers, including Xie Daoyun and her brother Xie Xuan. Under his influence, Daoyun developed similar character traits and a kindred style of personal behaviour. From the various anecdotes in the *Jin shu* and the *Shishuo xinyu* concerning Xie An and the younger generation, we form the impression that, among all the nephews and nieces, he favoured her and showed a special concern for her. About 360, Xie Daoyun married Wang Ningzhi. Ningzhi was from the Wang clan which enjoyed equal fame with the Xie clan, and his father was the famous calligrapher Wang Xizhi. The first time Daoyun returned to her natal home after her marriage, she expressed great dissatisfaction with her new husband:

> After becoming Wang Ningzhi's wife, Madame Xie went to the Wang Family, she viewed Ningzhi with great disdain. When she returned to the Xie home, she was greatly dissatisfied. The Grand Tutor (Xie An) comforted her saying, "Young Wang is the son of Yishao (Wang Xizhi); he himself is not bad either. Why are you so unhappy?" She replied, "I have as my father and uncles Ada (Xie Yi) and Zhonglang (Xie Wan); and as my brothers and cousins I have Feng (Xie Shao), Hu (Xie Lang), E (Xie Xuan) and Mo (Xie Yuan). I never imagined that a man like Master Wang could exist between heaven and earth."[20]

She compared Wang Ningzhi with the most distinguished members from the two generations of her own family and found him to be lacking miserably. Because of pride in her own talent and accomplishment, as well as in her family status, she easily found fault with others. In Wang Ningzhi's biography in *Jin shu*, he was said to have been accomplished in calligraphy of the *li* and the cursive styles. So he must have inherited his father's talent and achieved a high standard as a calligrapher. Besides, three fragments of his writing are preserved in the *Quan Jin wen:* "Poetic Essay on the Wind", "The impeachment of Fan Ning" and a letter. They all show good literary style. The "Poetic Essay on the Wind" is especially outstanding. Although only a few couplets have survived, they show a fresh and forceful style, not something that is made up of common literary clichés. In his official career he did quite well: he had been Prefect of Jiangzhou, Left General and Administrator of Kuaiji. From the point of view of clan prestige, the Wang clan was actually even slightly higher than the Xie clan. The Wang clan was older, and at the time of Daoyun's marriage, more prosperous than the Xie clan. From the early years of Western Jin, Wang Xiang and Wang Lan already enjoyed great fame, followed by Wang Rong and Wang Yan who were not only political leaders, but were highly influential in the intellectual world. Wang Dao, the first prime minister of the Eastern Jin court in the South, also came from this clan. During the early years of Eastern Jin, his position could almost equal the emperor himself. In addition, his

---

[20] *Shishuo xinyu jiaojian*, XIX, 26.

cousin Wang Dun controlled military power at the time, as seen above in the discussion of Xie Kun's carrier. The prestige of the Wang clan was such that there was a saying at the time, "The Wangs and the Mas (Sima, the surname of the Jin Imperial House) share the empire". However, during the latter part of Eastern Jin, the prestige of the Wang family dropped slightly. On the other hand, the Xie clan, once looked upon as a "new family",[21] by the latter part of Eastern Jin, reached the heights of its influence under the leadership of Xie An.

Nevertheless, Wang Ningzhi did have his weaknesses. From his biography we know that he was a fanatic believer of the Five-peck-of-rice Sect of Daoism to the degree of absurdity or even stupidity. We will give the details at a later stage. Suffice it to say here that Xie Daoyun's disappointment with her newly wed husband did not entirely stem from her own arrogance.

After her marriage, she continued to enjoy a considerable degree of freedom. An incident recorded in her biography in the *Jin shu* indicates that:

> Once Ningzhi's younger brother Xianzhi was having a discourse with his guests, and was on the verge of losing the argument when Daoyun sent a maidservant to Xianzhi, saying, "I would like to break the siege for the young master." She then hid behind a green silk screen and extended Xianzhi's original argument. None of the guests could defeat her.[22]

Among Ningzhi's brothers, Xianzhi was the most brilliant, and he was also respected as a "famous scholar". It was likely that his guests were also outstanding scholars yet none of them was able to defeat Daoyun, proving her excellence as a debater. This anecdote reveals that Daoyun was not afraid of showing her talent. She did not feel obliged to stay in the women's quarters all the time. If it pleased her, she would participate in an all male discussion. We can imagine that in ancient China many a woman had eavesdropped behind a screen on their men's conversations, and many a woman would have been anxious to try her own skill at activities such as philosophical discourse which were considered the sacrosanct realm of men; but how many of them dared to challenge tradition head on? Perhaps Xie Daoyun had absolute confidence in her own special status and was certain that her behaviour would not be criticized. Perhaps she would have done as she pleased caring little about whether or not she would be criticized. It is my opinion that both may be true. In her age—the Wei-Jin period—those who showed disregard for convention were usually praised for independence of spirit. Men whose behaviour was ten times more bizarre than hers were commended, hence a woman taking part in a philosophical discourse probably did not appear too shocking. She was a member of the Xie clan and married to a member of the Wang clan,

---

21 *Shishuo xinyu jiaojian*, XXIV, 9.
22 *Jin shu*, j. 96, p. 2516.

so it was likely that whatever she did was acceptable, and even superior. As a matter of fact, we have not been able to find any unfavourable criticism of her by her contemporaries. The inclusion of her biography in the chapter on eminent women, and further, to give a good coverage to the above incident, seems to indicate that her behaviour was considered praiseworthy in the light of the social standards of her time and even until the Tang dynasty when the *Jin shu* was compiled.

Perhaps because of Daoyun's intellectual brilliance, she tended to be impatient with other people and was often critical of others. Her criticism of her husband has been mentioned earlier. Her biography also includes her criticism of her younger brother Xie Xuan. She once mocked Xuan for not advancing in his learning with the words: "Is it because you are preoccupied with worldly matters or is it because you are limited by your potential?"[23] We have no way of telling when this comment was made or what provoked Daoyun's criticism, but Xie Xuan should be a brother to be proud of whatever measurement one might wish to use. His official biography in *Jin shu* maintained that he was "capable of philosophical discourse and good at logic". In addition, he was a national hero whose actions were crucial in saving the country from invaders.

Xie Daoyun and her children went with Wang Ningzhi to Kuaiji when he was Administrator of that commandery. At that time there was a man named Sun En who led a religious movement which had a great following among the masses. They raised a force against the government and occupied many cities along the eastern seaboard of China, killing officials in charge. In 399 they spread to Kuaiji. The biography of Wang Ningzhi in the *Jin shu* says:

> The Wang family had followed the Five-peck-of-rice Sect of Daoism for generations; Ningzhi was especially fervent. When Sun En attacked Kuaiji, Ningzhi's subordinates and assistants begged him to prepare its defence. Ningzhi would not follow their advice. After going to his meditation room to pray, he said to the generals and lieutenants, "I have made supplications to the Great Dao, and have been promised spirit soldiers to come to my aid. The bandits will be destroyed automatically." Since he had not prepared any defence, he was subsequently murdered by Sun En.[24]

Wang Ningzhi's fanaticism reached absurd proportions and led to the unnecessary deaths of himself and his sons. In contrast, Daoyun's behaviour on this tragic occasion was calm and dignified, as can be seen from her biography:

> When she met with the catastrophe of Sun En, she conducted herself as usual. When she heard that her husband and sons were murdered by the

---

[23] *Ibid.*, j. 96, p. 2516.
[24] *Ibid.*, j. 80, p. 2102.

bandits, she ordered her maids to carry her in a sedan chair and went out with drawn sword. Soon the insurgent soldiers began to come in. She killed several before she was taken prisoner. Her maternal grandson Liu Tao was only a few years old. The bandits wanted to kill him too. Daoyun said, "This is a matter concerning the Wang family, what has it to do with another clan? If you must do it, I'd rather be killed first." Though En was ruthless and cruel, he was moved by her, hence he did not kill Tao.[25]

Daoyun, already a grandmother at this time, demonstrates great courage by coming forth with a sword to kill her enemies. In order to protect her grandchild, she argued fearlessly with a plundering and ravaging pirate and made him change his mind.

After the death of her husband and sons, Daoyun led a widow's life in Kuaiji. She managed her household with stringent discipline. The Prefect of Kuaiji of that time was Liu Liu who, having heard of her reputation, asked to hold a philosophical discourse with her.

Daoyun had heard of Liu's name, so she did not restrain herself from this. Consequently, she put her hair in a bun and sat on a white cushion, behind curtains. Liu dressed himself neatly in formal attire, sat on another chair. Daoyun's words were pure and elegant, delivered in a lofty style. She started by talking about her family. Overwhelmed by emotion, she wept bitterly. Gradually she proceeded to answer his queries relating to philosophy, never hesitating or short of words or arguments. When Liu had taken his leave, he sighed and said, "She is really a lady like none I have ever known. Having heard her words and observed her style, one cannot help but admire her, body and soul." Daoyun also said, "After the death of my relations, I met this scholar. It is heartening to hear the questions he asked."[26]

This discourse was different from the one in which she saved Wang Xianzhi from verbal defeat. This time, none of her male relatives was present and as a widow she talked with a total stranger, an act breaking all the rules of propriety in traditional China, despite the fact that she was already a woman in her fifties or sixties. Her friendship with Liu Liu can be viewed as a union of intellect and spirit beyond the demarcation of age and gender.

There is one other record of Daoyun's philosophical discourse with another of her contemporaries which possibly took place also late in her life. It is referred to in a commentary of the *Shishuo xinyu*:

It was recorded in the *Furen ji* (Collected works of women) that once Huan Xuan asked Wang Ningzhi's wife née Xie, saying, "The Grand Tutor lived [as a recluse] at Dongshan for more than twenty years, yet he could not go through with it. What was the reason?" Xie answered, "My late uncle simply had non-utilitarianism as his principle. To be reclusive or to be prominent—the one is neither superior nor inferior to the other. What he

25 *Ibid.*, j. 96, p. 2516.
26 *Ibid.*, j. 96, pp. 2516-7.

did earlier and what he did later differed only in that one was the active and one the non-active [expression of the same principle].[27]

The reasons we attribute this dialogue to a period late in her life are: firstly, she referred to Xie An as "my late uncle", hence it had to take place after 385, the year in which Xie An died. Secondly, even though several members of the Xie family had been subordinates of Huan Wen, Huan Xuan's father, after Xie An emerged as the leader of the loyalists, the Huan clan and the Xie clan became opposing camps as noted earlier and there was a great deal of animosity between the two. After the death of the two patriarchs, there is no record of social relations between the two clans, hence the dialogue above could not have taken place in a social context. If we assume that their meeting had been requested by Huan Xuan (unlike the case of Liu Liu), in view of the situation at that time, Daoyun would not have consented to a discourse. Our assumption is based on the animosity between the two clans, as well as the fact that Huan Xuan's intention to follow his father's footsteps in usurping the Jin throne was blatant. Moreover, except for the short interval when he was Prefect of Yixing, Huan was in Jingzhou (present day Hubei) most of the time, thousands of miles from Kuaiji. Even when he began his military revolt, he fought around the provinces of Jingzhou and Jiangzhou (present day Jiangxi). It was only after he had defeated the Jin army that he moved east to the capital Jiankang. That was the year 402. He usurped the throne the next year and was defeated and killed by Liu Yu in the following year. Therefore, we assume that his dialogue with Daoyun took place in the year or so after he arrived at the capital, or after he had usurped the throne, and thereby had the prerogative to call Daoyun for an audience. After Huan Xuan gained power, he often liked to compare himself with the idols of "famous scholars" such as Xie An and Wang Xianzhi,[28] and he would ask others how he compared with Xie and Wang. Those he interrogated, though intimidated, did not give him the answer he desired. Consequently, he was always looking for opportunities to downgrade Xie An's reputation. Both *Shishuo xinyu* and *Jin shu* record that he wanted to use Xie An's former residence as barracks, and only gave up the idea when the latter's grandson protested.[29] Stemming from the same motive, in this anecdote, he seemed to want to focus on Xie An's inability to go through with his aspiration of being a lifelong recluse in order to embarrass Daoyun.

Usually, the record of philosophical discourses of the *Shishuo xinyu* and *Jin shu* are limited to a description of the situation and who had the upper hand; only rarely do they record details of the discourse or debate.

---

[27] *Shishuo xinyu jiaojian*, XXV, 26, commentary. I suspect *wei* (verb to be) in *xian yin wei you lie* is an error for *wu* (void).

[28] Examples of his sounding out others concerning how he would compare with Xie and Wang can be seen in *Shishuo xinyu jiaojian*, IX, 86 and 87.

[29] *Shishuo xinyu jiaojian*, X, 27 and *Jin shu*, j. 79, p. 2079.

Among the three entries which report Daoyun's philosophical discourses, neither the one about her helping Wang Xianzhi to win an argument, nor the one about her meeting with Liu Liu give us any of the arguments themselves; only the third one quotes her repartee. This anecdote gives us some indication of Daoyun's thinking. On the one hand she lauds Xie An's Daoist tendency of non-utilitarianism, on the other, in her view, neither being reclusive nor being prominent is necessarily the criterion for judging the superiority of a scholar. She thereby makes a compromise with the Confucian idea of "participation in worldly affairs". In fact, from its inception, *xuanxue* had been a syncretic school encompassing more than one school of thought. It maintained that Daoism and Confucianism (later scholars added Buddhism) were actually different sides of the same truth. This tendency in her thinking must also have roots in the traditions of the Xie family. The Xie clan were reputable Confucian specialists and yet Xie Kun, Xie Shang, Xie An and Xie Wan were all known for their Daoist thinking and behaviour. Therefore, Daoyun's assessment of her uncle Xie An was based on a syncretic viewpoint which looked upon the difference between "being reclusive" and "being prominent" as minimal. They were only the unimportant outward expressions. What was important was Xie An's principle of non-utilitarianism.

How much longer she lived after that we have no way of knowing, but the date of her death must have been after 399, because that was the year Sun En killed her husband. If we assume her dialogue with Huan Xuan took place after the latter gained power or usurped it, then her death must have taken place after 404. In any case, she lived to about the age of sixty. She seems to have had quite a few children. The previous quotation from her biography in *Jin shu* states that "she heard that her husband and sons (*zhu zi*) had been murdered by the bandits." The use of *zhu* indicates that she had at least three sons. Since she had a maternal grandson (*waisun*), she must have had at least one daughter who had married into the Liu family. Moreover, in *Quan Jin wen*, there is a letter by Wang Ningzhi, written to the "daughter married to Yu". So it is possible that another daughter had married into the Yu family. Of course, we must not rule out the possibility that this daughter could have been borne by a concubine.

We learn from Daoyun's biography in *Jin shu* that "her poems, poetic essays, eulogies and odes circulated among her contemporaries."[30] The folowing entry is to be found in the bibliographic chapter of *Sui shu*: "Collected works of Xie Daoyun, wife of Wang Ningzhi, Prefect of Jiangzhou of the Jin dynasty, 2 volumes".[31] Obviously, when the *Sui shu* was compiled in the Tang dynasty, her collected works were still extant. The bibliographical

---

[30] *Jin shu*, j. 96, p. 2517.
[31] *Sui shu*, j. 35, p. 1070.

chapters of both the *Jiu Tang shu* and the *Xin Tang shu,* compiled during the Song dynasty, no longer list any of her works. Therefore, it must have been during the latter part of Tang or the Five Dynasties that her collection was lost. What are now left are the fragments culled from various encyclopaedias and collected in the anthologies *Quan Jin wen* and *Quan Jin shi.* With the exception of one of the poetry fragments which consists of only one line, the rest are translated below:

"Ascending a Mountain"

How lofty is the eastern mountain,
Majestic and reaching to the sky.
Inside the cliffs an imagined dwelling stands,
Lonely, remote and ethereal.
Not by the hands of workers nor craftsmen,
The cloud-reaching structure was born of nature.
How splendid is thy aura,
That my thoughts often thither wander.
When I go, I shall in this dwelling reside,
And live out the remainder of my natural years.

"Emulating Grand Master Xi's 'Ode to a Pine'"[32]

Watching from afar a pine on the mountain,
In severe winter its leaves do not fall,
How I wish to rest under it during my excursion,
And look up to its branches extending thousands of feet.
I leapt high, but failed to fly,
So I stamp my foot and wait for Wang Qiao.[33]
But time does not wait for me,
I shall be carried away by the gale of fate.

[The two poems above are in *Quan Jin shi* compiled by Ding Fubao.]

"In Praise of the *Lunyu*"

Duke Ling of Wei asked Confucius about battle formation, Confucius said, "I have heard of matters concerning sacrificial rites, but I have never studied matters concerning the army." This is magnificent! It can be compared to *Zhongyong* in virtue. These words are so sound that on their account everyone regards him as a teacher. People who neglect them shall not find the source of truth; but those who understand them well shall have a good end. O my thoughts, they are in total agreement with his words. Confucius said, "Benevolence is more vital to the people than water or fire. I have seen people die because of water or fire, but I have never seen anyone die because of benevolence."

---

[32] Xi Kang's full official title is Grand Master of Palace Leisure. The poem in question is possibly the one entitled "Youxian shi", in *Xi zhongsan ji*, j. 1, p. 5b.

[33] An immortal.

[The above is found in *Quan Jin wen*, compiled by Yan Kejun of the Qing dynasty.]

Daoyun's literary works which we are able to read now are not of the highest calibre. However, both from the view of style and content, they do not fall into the traditional stereotype of works by women writers. The two poems "Ascending a Mountain" and "Emulating Grand Master Xi's 'Ode to a Pine'" are very similar to the *Youxian shi* (Quest for immortals) genre of poetry popular at the time, which was mainly concerned with living as a recluse and aspiring to be an immortal, and had strong Daoist undertones.

The poem "Emulating Grand Master Xi's 'Ode to a Pine'" shows Daoyun's profound influence by the group already known as the "Seven Worthies of the Bamboo Grove" in her time. Xi refers to Xi Kang, one of the most prominent members of this group. The poem resembles closely one of Xi Kang's entitled "Youxian shi" (Quest for Immortals) not only in spirit but even in diction. For the sake of comparison, an excerpt of Xi's poem is included below:

"Quest for Immortals"

Watching from afar a pine on the mountain
Prominent in a valley lush and green
How lofty it holds itself,
Standing alone, none could be its match,
How I wish to play under it,
But no path can be found leading there,
Wang Qiao deserts and leaves me;
So I ride the clouds on a six-dragon carriage.
A gale carries me to play in the Black Garden,
On the way I meet Huangdi and Laozi,
Who teach me the Way of Nature,
My enlightenment may be likened to that of the first day of a schoolboy.

Daoyun's affinity to this group of intellectuals can also be seen from a comment made by a contemporary:

Earlier, the sister of Zhang Xuan, who was from the same commandery, was also considered talented. She had married into the Gu family. Xuan often praised her and wanted to match her against Daoyun. There was the nun Ji who made frequent visits to both households. When asked [to evaluate the two], Nun Ji said, "Lady Wang's expression is relaxed and open, therefore she has the style of the Seven Worthies of the Bamboo Grove; while Gu's wife has a pure heart like a piece gleaming jade, and quite naturally is an outstanding example among women.[34]

She said Zhang Xuan's sister had a "pure heart like a piece of gleaming jade", an attribute used often to describe intelligent women. It signifies that among women she was outstanding. But, to describe Xie, she used "relaxed and open", a description seldom applied to women.

---

[34] *Jin shu*, j. 66, p. 2517.

She went on to say that Daoyun "has the style of the Seven Worthies of the Bamboo Grove", comparing her with the ultimate heroes of "famous scholars". In view of the fact that this group symbolized the Daoist ideal, it was the highest tribute one could pay to any person, male or female. From this evaluation, Daoyun's eminence in the eyes of her contemporaries may be clearly seen.

In a way, Daoyun's "In Praise of the *Lunyu*" can be viewed as a footnote to the Confucian roots of the Xie clan. It demonstrates her thorough familiarity and understanding of the Confucian ideals. Moreover, it can probably correct a mistaken impression people might have regarding Daoyun's philosophical outlook by showing us that her attention was not entirely preoccupied by Daoist thinking. She also studied and wrote about Confucian subjects.

From the information presented above concerning Xie Daoyun's life and work, it is possible to form certain impressions of her personality. On the philosophical side, we know that she had more than once participated in philosophical discourse. The subject of her discourse, among other things, included "character criticism", a topic which was popular and well-developed in her time. As far as her command of the technique and subject matter of philosophical discourse are concerned, she had shown that she measured up with the most illustrious members of her time and was often superior to them. From the three cases we know of, she had gained the upper hand in all of them. Especially in the one case in which she helped Wang Xianzhi to win an argument, she defeated all of the men who were present. As to her philosophical outlook, following some of the predecessors in her clan, by blending Confucianism and Daoism, she formulated her own syncretic philosophy. However, possibly due to her personality, her thinking has closer affinities with Daoism than Confucianism. The heights she reached in Daoist thinking can be seen from her philosophical discourses and written works and also from the way she deported herself in life.

In literature, we can detect from the anecdote in which she took part in impromptu oral poetry composition with Xie An and Xie Lang, that she had a quick mind and that her style was fresh and elegant, imbued with aesthetic qualities. It is a pity that in the two poems preserved in *Quan Jin shi*, few lines of that calibre can be found. But since most of her works are lost, we cannot really make a fair evaluation of her literary achievement. We are only able to conclude that her literary concerns are not confined to the usual "feminine" ones, such as natural beauty, love poems and loneliness, but follow the mainstream of the time with themes concerning the "quest for immortality" and metaphysics. Her "In Praise of the *Lunyu*" is academic, expounding and praising the thought of Confucius. Daoyun also showed great perception in literary criticism. In her dialogue with Xie An about the

Shijing, her admiration was not for the superficially pretty but for expressions of profound humanity.

Daoyun's biography in *Jin shu* emphasized her talent as the basis of her achievement in literature and philosophy. However, her personal effort and her special family background, especially the influence of her uncle Xie An, must be important factors as well. From her remonstration of her brother Xie Xuan for not continuing to grow in learning, we can see that she was a person never satisfied with the *status quo* but always demanding more from herself and others. This desire to always strive for a higher goal motivated her to work harder and advance. Daoyun's achievement in literature and scholarship is outstanding, but what is more unusual about her is her personal style. In spite of the temporary relaxation in the control of women, the society of her time was still basically patriarchal. In such a social environment she had the courage to say what she thought and act as she chose. A woman had no say in the choice of her husband, and once married, should accept him whatever he was like. The way she complained about Wang Ningzhi was most unusual. She was also outspoken in her criticism of her own brother. She did not hesitate to take part in the philosophical discourse of her brother-in-law. Neither did she show any false modesty on the occasion, and defeated everyone present. When she was a widow and wished to hold a philosophical discourse with a stranger she "did not restrain herself".

This kind of flagrant individualism is close to Xie An's. In Xie An's biography in *Jin shu*, he is said to have been criticized by his contemporaries for being extravagant as well as for listening to music during a mourning period,[35] but he "did not condescend to pay any notice". Both uncle and niece challenged contemporary codes of behaviour. This reveals their courage, but also their arrogance. Moreover, it shows their reluctance to be hypocritical, since it was an important Daoist virtue to be true to one's natural inclinations. Another characteristic in Daoyun's personal style is the ability to remain calm in the face of danger. The valour and the steely determination she displayed during her confrontation with Sun En and his followers are exceptionally admirable, whether in a man or a woman. She shared this characteristic with some of her ancestors. Xie An and Xie Kun also demonstrated the same qualities, the former when he walked open-eyed into the trap Huan Wen had set for him, and the latter, in his many confrontations with Wang Dun. Tracing the source of Daoyun's individualism and her personal courage, one might find it in a deep-seated commitment to Daoist philosophy. Because she disregarded personal glory and humiliation, so she was able to remain independent in thought and deed; because she equated life with death, so she was able to remain calm in the face of danger. Hence her

---

[35] *Ibid.*, j. 79, pp. 2075-6.

45

personality is inseparable from her philosophical perception. It is no wonder that the nun named Ji, when making a character criticism, described her in Daoist terms and put her in the same league as the Seven Worthies of the Bamboo Grove, who occupied the highest order in the hierarchy of "famous scholars" of the Six Dynasties.

Judging from the breadth of her interests and the respect she commanded among her contemporaries, of all the eminent women of traditional China only Ban Zhao can compare with Xie Daoyun. However, Ban Zhao's *Nüjie* reveals that she conformed closely with the patriarchal orthodoxy of her time and lacked the kind of independent thinking which Daoyun was able to maintain. Among the biographies in the chapter on eminent women of the *Jin shu*, several of them were not known for their virtue; they were selected because of their talent or perception. This can be seen as evidence that during that period, women's talents were admired as much as their virtue, contrary to the attitude of later eras that: "the lack of talent is a virtue in a woman". It was in such an enlightened atmosphere that it was possible for such an outstanding and unconventional woman as Xie Daoyun to flourish.

The Emergence of Buddhist Nuns in China and Its Social Ramifications

Though there are many different theories regarding the introduction of Buddhism into China, there is no doubt that by the end of the Han Dynasty it had already gained many believers and supporters in China. It is recorded in the *Gao seng zhuan* (Biographies of eminent monks), a sixth century work by Monk Huijiao,[1] that from the end of the reign of Emperor Ling of Han (168-189) Chinese monks were already in existence, though most of the monks included in chapters on the early periods in this book are from India and Central Asia. The appearance of nuns, foreign or Chinese, however, had to wait about one hundred and fifty years, until the Jin Dynasty, when Buddhism became more established in China. From the *Gao seng zhuan* we also see that in the early years, foreign monks, not indigenous ones, played the leading role in all aspects of Buddhist life. Judging from the *Biqiuni zhuan* (Biographies of the nuns), however, all eminent nuns in the early period were Chinese. The first foreign nuns came to China in the year 429,[2] more than a century after the first Chinese woman received the precepts and formed a convent.

Kathryn Ts'ai has provided Western readers with a comprehensive view of convent life in China.[3] Nancy Schuster Barnes has also pointed out some of the salient features of Chinese Buddhist nuns, such as their erudition and role as teachers.[4] This paper will look at the appearance of Chinese nuns as a social phenomenon. For a Chinese woman, to leave the home and live by herself in seclusion was contrary to the role assigned to her by tradition. To break free from such a tradition required tremendous courage and determination on the part of the individual and raises questions such as: What kind of women took this step and why? What changes, if any, did the appearance of nuns bring to medieval China? In order to answer these questions, I have tried to extract and analyse information on the lives of the thirteen nuns included in the first chapter of *Biqiuni zhuan* who were among the first women to receive the precepts in China (roughly from 312 to 420), as well as information relating to their family background, education level, marital status and temperament. The circumstances under which they were ordained, especially the difficulties they had to overcome, are also investigated here. Finally, the achievements of these women, both in religious and lay life, are set out and their influence on Chinese women

---

[1] Huijiao, *Gao seng zhuan* in *Dazang jing*, j. 1, 2b.

[2] *Biqiuni zhuan* in *Dazang jing*, j. 2, Biography 14.

[3] Kathryn Ann Ts'ai, "The Chinese Buddhist Monastic Order for Women: the First Two Centuries", Richard W. Guisso and Stanley Johannesen (eds), *Women in China: Current Directions in Historical Scholarship*, pp. 1-20.

[4] Nancy Schuster Barnes, "Buddhism", Arvind Sharma (ed.), *Women in World Religions*, p. 128.

and Chinese society as a whole is assessed. My reasons for confining this study to only the nuns of the first chapter is because I believe these thirteen nuns were innovators who pioneered a new kind of life heretofore unknown in China and that their actions established most of the models which nuns of future generations emulated.

The most important source for the study of Chinese nuns is the *Biqiuni zhuan* written by Baochang, a monk who flourished at the end of the fifth and the beginning of the sixth century. He is also the compiler of a number of other important Buddhist biographies and bibliographies, including *Ming seng ji* (Biographies of well-known monks) and *Zhong jing mulu* (Catalogue of *sutras*). The *Biqiuni zhuan* had been passed over by scholars until recently, when Kathryn Cissell submitted a Ph.D. thesis in 1972[5] on this work. Her thesis consists of a study of the work and a complete translation of the text. My information for this paper has mainly come from the *Biqiuni zhuan*, using the original Chinese text, as I find sometimes that my understanding of this text differs from that of Dr Cissell. Whenever possible, other sources, such as the *Jin shu*, the dynastic history covering this period, and other non-Buddhist records, were consulted in order to substantiate or augment the information therein. Even so, one must realize that the data in the *Biqiuni zhuan* can only help us discover certain trends of the period concerned, and that they cannot be looked upon as historical facts. After all, it was written by a Buddhist scholar in order to glorify his religion.

There are many complicated arguments as to who was the first nun in China. Cissell's thesis provides us with an exhaustive examination of this question. Her conclusion, it seems to me, is inclined to agree with Baochang in according Jingjian (fl. first half of 4th century) the honour of being the first Chinese nun. As far as this chapter is concerned, this question is not important because even if nuns did exist before Jingjian, no information about their lives has survived. The thirteen nuns whose biographies are found in Baochang's *Biqiuni zhuan* may not be the first nuns, but they are generally considered as representative members of the Chinese *biksuni* of the earliest period.

In this initial period when women intended to withdraw from home life and become nuns, they encountered a number of difficulties, the foremost being the lack of information concerning the laws and precepts which they were to learn and practise. When Jingjian first read in the *sutra* that there was a female branch of the *sangha* (Buddhist order) she was interested in learning more of it, but her enquiries for further details were not satisfactorily answered. Her eagerness to become a nun was so great that she decided to receive the precepts on an incomplete knowledge of the laws, thus putting the validity of her

---

[5] Kathryn Ann Adelsperger Cissell, "The *Pi-ch'iu-ni chuan*: Biographies of Famous Chinese Nuns from 317-516 CE" (Ph. D. thesis, University of Wisconsin, 1972).

own ordination and that of those who followed her, in doubt. Yet that did not seem to stop the number of nuns from growing rapidly, as most of the convents of this period mentioned in the *Biqiuni zhuan* had a population of more than one hundred.[6]

In later eras some nuns left family life as a result of their parents' wishes. There were those who went into the convent because they suffered bad health, as it was believed that if they devoted themselves to a pure and pious life, their health would improve. There were even cases where babies were pledged to a monastery or a convent before birth.[7] However, all of the women in our study became nuns voluntarily, mostly out of religious zeal. They were all at least young adults when they made the decision, usually after a fairly long period of self-imposed austerity and vegetarian diet as well as self-study of Buddhist teachings. The most vehement resistance to a woman's wish to enter the convent usually came from parents, stemming from the traditional view that the happiest and most proper future for a young woman was to be married to a suitable husband. In the case of An Lingshou, there was a head-on confrontation between the two generations:

> Her father said, "You should [eventually] be married into another family. How can you continue like this. Shou said, "I have set my mind on the Buddhist truth and consider it my life-long career, renouncing all human relationships. Being self-contained in my purity and integrity, I cannot be moved by either praise or criticism. Why must I conform to the 'three attachments'[8] before being considered within propriety?" Her father said, "You only care about your own welfare, how can you help your parents at the same time?" Shou replied, "I am determined to practise the laws exactly because I have a desire to help liberate all beings, how much more my own parents?"[9]

This debate between father and daughter clearly pitches the Confucian virtue of *renlun*, orderly human relationships, against an individual's right to seek truth and spiritual liberation. In the Confucian tradition, a woman should, at every stage of her life, be attached to a male member of the family, hence the "three attachments" referred to in An's conversation with her father. Her outright refutation of this Confucian

---

[6] In Tanbei's biography, the number of Jingjian's disciples is said to have been three hundred; for Sengji and Miaoyin, more than one hundred.

[7] Li Ruzhen, *Jing hua yuan*, p. 73. Although *Jing hua yuan* is a work of fiction, it is generally acknowledged to contain Li Ruzhen's serious criticism of Chinese society.

[8] *Sancong* is usually translated as the "three submissions", but E. T. Williams, in his *China Yesterday and Today*, has translated *cong* as "to follow", in the physical sense, hence a woman should be attached to her father's household when she was not married, to her husband's when she married and to her son's when her husband died.

[9] *Biqiuni zhuan*, j. 1, Biography 2.

tenet amounts to a declaration of independence for Chinese women. To break away from this tradition was already considered improper, but to act against one's father's wishes, for woman and man alike, was the greatest sin one could commit—the sin of being unfilial. Yet from An's argument, we see that she was putting the Buddhist duty of seeking liberation from the pains of karma above the Confucian duty of obeying and serving one's parents. It is not possible to predict how this conflict would have ended if Fotu Cheng, a prominent Buddhist monk, had not intervened. According to *Biqiuni zhuan*, Cheng performed a miracle through which An's father was able to see that his daughter was actually a Buddhist monk in another incarnation and hence agreed to her ordination.

In another case the conflict was between mother and daughter, although the events were not less dramatic. Sengji's mother would not allow her to become a nun; she had secretly promised her in marriage, but had hidden the engagement gifts from her. When Sengji found out about it she went on a hunger strike until she was on the brink of death. The groom-to-be was so moved by her unwavering commitment that he voluntarily gave up his claim on her. Thus the would-be tragedy turned out to have a happy ending in which all the friends and relatives came with expensive presents and offerings to congratulate her on her ordination. Even the head of the commandery came in person. It was described as an historical occasion by observers. The warm reception of Sengji's relatives and the head of the commandery seem to indicate that from the time of An Lingshou (fl. c. 335) to the time of Sengji's ordination (350), attitudes had already become more moderate.

In Minggan's case the resistance came from her husband and children. Minggan was captured by marauding non-Chinese tribesmen and kept a prisoner for an extended period. When she finally returned home after great hardship and a dangerous escape, she had made up her mind to live a religious life. But her family prevented her from fulfilling her wish for three years. When she continued to persist in her practice of religious ways at home, she was finally allowed to devote her life exclusively to Buddhism.

The family name and native place of all the nuns are given in their biographies in *Biqiuni zhuan* except for one whose family history is said to be unknown. Out of the twelve with familial details, at least five came from families of the official class: Jingjian, An Lingshou, Zhixian, Miaoxiang and Daoyi. The others, judging from details provided in their biographies, also seem to come from at least middle-class backgrounds, although no explicit information is actually given.

A rare visual image of early Chinese nuns found in the murals of the caves of Dunhuang.

We have seen above the kind of familial resistance women had to face. In some isolated cases parents were less autocratic. For example, Tanbei's mother understood the futility of her own objection and let her daughter have her wish. Two of the nuns, Jingjian and Daoyi, were widowed when they were still young. Minggan and Miaoxiang were both married women. Minggan's story has been recounted above and Miaoxiang's case is extraordinary for the times in which she lived. Miaoxiang was married to a young man of high social standing, a secretary to the Heir-Apparent, but divorced him on the grounds of his improper behaviour during a mourning period, and subsequently became a nun. Her father approved both actions. This was one of the very few instances where a woman initiated a divorce in traditional China.

Geographically, the thirteen nuns came from widely scattered places; from Shandong, Shanxi, Henan in the north to Jiangsu and Zhejiang in the south. However, because the age they lived in was one of upheaval and turmoil, some of them ended up far away from their native homes. For example, Daoyi was born in the Loufan district of Yanmen commandery which is east of Dunxian in modern Shanxi province, but in her old age she resided in the He Hou Convent in the southern capital of Jiankang (modern Nanjing) and died there. It is to be noted that the convents to which our subjects were attached were located in or near two centres: Luoyang and Jiankang. Luoyang in the north, was the capital of Eastern Han when Buddhism was first introduced to China and continued to be the capital until Western Jin. In this centre three convents were located in the capital itself; another two convents in Sizhou, the capital territory; and one in Hongnong, which was in the same commandery as Luoyang. The second centre was Jiankang, the capital of Eastern Jin, in which six convents were located. It is interesting, therefore, to note that women whose native places were far apart converged on two centres which no doubt were the religious hearts of Buddhism in that age. It is worth pointing out also that in this early period, the proportion of nuns from the north was very high: six nuns lived in the north and there were two who had migrated to Jiankang from the north. This was, of course, due to the fact that Buddhism was introduced to the north-west of China first, and moved gradually to the south-east. The development of the history of Chinese nuns followed the same pattern.

As Cissell has pointed out, the nuns whose lives are recorded in the *Biqiuni zhuan*, were selected for inclusion "to provide examples of great virtue in a degenerate age".[10] In fact, their achievements went far beyond virtue and encompassed a wide spectrum of activities. What qualities can be said to have characterized these nuns who distinguished

---

[10] Cissell, "Preface", *op. cit.*, p. ii.

themselves in this early history of Buddhist nuns? We might find answers by analysing some of their personal charactersitics.

The quality that was essential for the emergence of Chinese nuns was initiative. This was displayed amply by Jingjian, generally recognized as the first Chinese woman to become a nun. The circumstances of her ordination are important enough to warrant a quotation from the *Biqiuni zhuan*:

> Later she met the Monk Fashi, who was well versed in the Buddhist *sutras* and philosophy. He had established a temple at the Western Gate of the Palace in the middle of the Jianxian period (313-317), Jian hence went to see him. He then expounded the law for her, consequently Jian experienced a great awakening. She wished to reach a stronger understanding in order to seek the benefit of the *dharma*. She borrowed *sutras* from [Fa]shi, from these she grasped the principles [of Buddhism]. Another day, she said to [Fa]shi, "It is written in the *sutras: bhiksus* and *bhiksunis* wish to reach the state of liberation." [Fa]shi answered, "In the West, there are two orders, but in this land, we do not yet have the rules [for nuns]." Jian said, "Since it says *bhiksus* and *bhiksunis*, how can they have different rules?" [Fa]shi said, "Foreigners say that nuns have five hundred precepts, so they must be different. I should ask an instructor for you." The instructor said, "The precepts for nuns are mostly the same, with minor differences, but without the rules, you cannot be taught. However, there are ten precepts for nuns which can be received from an eminent monk, but without an instructor-nun, you will have no-one to depend upon." Jian shaved her hair immediately, and received the ten precepts from the instructor. Twenty-four others also shared her aspiration. Together they established the Zhulin Convent near the West Gate of the Palace City. In the absence of an instructor-nun, they all consulted Jian.[11]

From this quotation it is clear Jingjian took the initiative throughout. In a society in which women had always passively followed a traditional pattern and obeyed the biddings of men, she had the initiative and courage to break free and embark on a completely unprecedented life. Jingjian became a nun not at the urging of a male religious mentor; she was clearly the one who thought of the idea; she was the one who wanted to find out more about the procedures. Despite the uncertainties involved with the rules and the lack of a female instructor, she decisively cut her hair and received the ten precepts from the Indian monk Zhishan, and embarked upon an exclusively religious life. Together with the other women who were ordained with her she founded the first recorded convent in China and virtually acted as their instructor-nun.

A trait common to all these women is perhaps their high level of intelligence and spiritual perception. From the quotation above we learned that after Jingjian had heard Fashi expound the Buddhist philosophy only once, she was able to understand the principles of

---

[11] *Biqiuni zhuan*, j. 1, Biography 1.

Buddhism by studying *sutras* borrowed from him. An Lingshou is said to have "read widely in all subjects, and whatever she set her eyes upon, she was sure to be able to recite. Her thinking was profound while her perception was capable of reaching the remote and distant."[12]

Miaoxiang is described in these words: "When her mind travelled in the realm of the wise Commentaries [to the *sutras* and *vinayas*] she clearly comprehended the characteristics of the dharma."[13] When Lingzong "opened up the *sutras* to read, her deep perception entered the realm of the spirit";[14] and Daoyi is described as "intelligent, with a quick and philosophical mind. She had a wide knowledge and an excellent memory... With intuitive perception she grasped the essence and meaning of [Buddhist philosophy]."[15]

Debating talent and analytical power were valued highly during the Wei-Jin period among intellectuals in general, as they were indispensable qualifications for participating in philosophical discourse, an activity which formed an essential part of the literati's life. The nuns had their illustrious examples in this category, too, in the persons of Zhu Daoxing and Miaoxiang. Zhu was said to have been "competent in philosophical discourse; she was especially good in the Hinayana school of Buddhist thought. She valued logical reasoning rather than the use of rhetoric and debating techniques."[16] Miaoyin "frequently held gatherings with the Emperor, the Grand Tutor and scholars of the court in which they discussed philosophy or composed literary works. She had a great reputation because of her talent."[17] Daoyi could expound the *Vimalakirti Sūtra* and the Lesser (or Smaller) *Prajñaparamita*.[18]

Still others were said to have been gifted administrators. For instance, according to *Biqiuni zhuan*, Tanbei's disciple Tanluo had a talent for careful and thorough administration; she planned and executed building programmes of considerable size.[19] Another of the nuns, Sengji, was a "most thorough administrator and was good at discussing matters and issues so that Emperor Kang treated her with admiration and respect. In the second year of Jianyan (344) Empress Chu established a convent named Yanxing Convent in Duting Alley in Tonggong Lane; Ji was in charge of its more than one hundred members. She was just and wise when managing the affairs of the convent."[20]

---

12 *Ibid.*, j. 1, Biography 2.
13 *Ibid.*, j. 1, Biography 4.
14 *Ibid.*, j. 1, Biography 11.
15 *Ibid.*, j. 1, Biography 13.
16 *Ibid.*, j. 1, Biography 9.
17 *Ibid.*, j. 1, Biography 12.
18 *Ibid.*, j. 1, Biography 13.
19 *Ibid.*, j. 1, Biography 6.
20 *Ibid.*, j. 1, Biography 8.

Unusual moral courage and endurance is another of their common characteristics. Three of the women resisted fearlessly men who would rob them of their chastity. One of them, Zhixian, was stabbed twenty times and left for dead.[21] Another, Minggan, captured by marauding tribesmen, was forced to serve as a shepherdess for ten years, until finally she decided to run away. She was said to have been guided by a tiger when she lost her way in the mountains, before finally reaching the safety of home.[22] We have seen above the courageous examples of Sengji and An Lingshou in their fight against the institution of marriage and parental pressure. The kind of courage required to go against a tradition which was centuries old is probably no less significant than the kind that is required to protect one's chastity in the face of danger and hardship.

It is probable that all nuns received some kind of education, either before or during their convent life; they must at least have been taught the *sutras*. Kathryn Ts'ai found that of all the nuns included in the *Biqiuni zhuan* over eighty per cent were literate.[23] Of the thirteen nuns in our study, and the disciple of one of them, only the biographies of two of them do not mention studying, or at least reciting some *sutra* or other, suggesting that at least eighty-five percent of them had some kind of learning. In Tanbei's biography no mention is made either, but in the biography of her disciple Tanluo which is attached to hers, Tanluo is described as being widely read in the *sutras* and *vinayas*, hence it would probably be safe to assume that her teacher, Tanbei, was educated also. Three of the nuns, Jingjian, An Lingshou and Miaoxiang, were said to have been fond of studying when they were young and from the sequence of the narration, in all three cases, this love was displayed before they entered the convent. These were women who entered the convent at a mature age and were from families of fairly high social status where they presumably received an education. That the convent provided some kind of education is borne out in the biography of Zhu Daoxing:

> When she was a novice, running errands for everyone, she was constantly reciting the *sutras*. When she was twenty, she could recite *sutras* such as the Lotus and the *Vimalakirti*. After she received the precepts, she studied and sought for the satisfaction of reaching the truth.[24]

If this could be taken as a common pattern in convent life, then it is possible to assume that when young novices first entered the convent they were charged with the duty of running errands for the nuns, but at

---

21 *Ibid.*, j. 1, Biography 3.
22 *Ibid.*, j. 1, Biography 5.
23 Ts'ai, *op. cit.,* p. 12.
24 *Biqiuni zhuan*, j. 1, Biography 9.

the same time they were taught the *sutras*. The intelligent and hard-working ones could continue to study after they had been ordained.

One element common to most biographies of religious personalities is the inclusion of some events in which the subject displays some supernatural insight or power. In the *Biqiuni zhuan* this element is also present, but not to the point of causing the reader to eye all information in the biographies with scepticism. However, many of the nuns portrayed had had miraculous events happen to them. One of them, Daorong, was even said to have been a saint. To test the validity of her sainthood, Emperor Ming of Jin placed flowers underneath her mat. The flowers remained uncrushed after she sat on the mat. She was also believed to have created a giant spirit in the form of a Buddhist monk which filled a Daoist retreat in Emperor Jianwen's palace, as well as having been responsible for getting rid of a nest of inauspicious crows for the same emperor. Her end was also shrouded in mystery: she just disappeared leaving her robe and her bowl. Two nuns, Minggan and Lingzong, are said to have been saved miraculously by animals, a tiger and a deer respectively, when in danger. Huizhan was also saved by a miracle: when a robber wanted to kill her, he could not lift his knife. Jingjian and Lingzong both had strange visions before their deaths. Jingjian's death is portrayed in the following account:

> At the end of the Shengping era (357-361), she smelled again the fragrance which she had smelt before.[25] She also saw a red aura. A woman holding flowers of five different colours descended from the sky. Jian saw it and rejoiced. Hence she said to the others, "Manage well the affairs after me. I am leaving presently." She held their hands to bid them farewell, and rose in the air, leaving a rainbow-like trail reaching straight into the sky.[26]

Compared with the biographies in the later chapters of the *Biqiuni zhuan*, the hagiographic tendency of this first chapter is far less marked.

While in convents, nuns developed vocations according to their talents and interests. As mentioned earlier, the nuns whose biographies appear in the *Biqiuni zhuan* were chosen because of their fame and achievements. From the lives of the thirteen nuns in our study we find that the areas in which nuns, and hence women as nuns, at that time, could endeavour to achieve excellence are as indicated below.

Scholarship: Many of the nuns were said to have been learned, but a few especially distinguished themselves as Buddhist scholars. We have already discussed the intellectual ability of some of them, such as An Lingshou, Zhu Daoxing and Miaoyin. Their talent and love for learning had won them prestige in the eyes of not only the community of nuns, but also the Buddhist community at large. Both An Lingshou

---

[25] When Jingjian was re-ordained, a fragrance filled the air which could be smelled by everyone present. See *Biqiuni zhuan*, j. 1, Biography 1.

[26] *Ibid.*, j. 1, Biography 1.

and Zhu Daoxing are recorded in the *Biqiuni zhuan* as teachers esteemed by all the Buddhist scholars of their times. Zhu Daoxing was also the first nun to acquire sufficient stature to expound the *sutras*,[27] a privilege reserved only for the masters, even amongst monks. Zhi Miaoyin "studied extensively Buddhist and non-Buddhist texts, and was good at composition. Emperor Xiaowu of Jin, the Grand Tutor—the Prince of Kuaiji [Sima] Dao[zi], Meng Yi and others all respected her. Often she would hold discussions and write compositions with the Emperor as well as the Grand Tutor and the courtiers."[28] When Daoyi travelled from Xunyang (present day Jiangxi) to Jiankang in the Taiyuan period (376-396), it was because she had heard that in the area of the capital, the *sutras* and *vinayas* were gradually being introduced and that lectures and meetings were being held one after the other. While she was there she lived in the He Hou Convent and set her mind on the *Vinaya-pitaka* and studied them until she clearly understood the fine points therein.[29] Some nuns were said to have been accomplished exponents of *qingtan* (philosophical discourse). The cases of Daoxing and Miaoyin already quoted from *Biqiuni zhuan*, are also borne out by both the official histories as well as *biji xiaoshuo* writings of the day. The following story about a nun making a comparison of two well-known ladies of the time appears both in the *Jin shu* and *Shishuo xinyu*[30] with only very minor variations. Here we quote the *Jin shu*:

> Earlier, the sister of Zhang Xuan who was from the same commandery, was also considered talented. She had married into the Gu family. Xuan often praised her and wanted to match her against Daoyun. There was the nun Ji who made frequent visits to both households. When asked [to evaluate the two], Nun Ji said, "Lady Wang's expression is relaxed and open, therefore she has the style of the Seven Worthies of the Bamboo Grove; while Gu's wife has a pure heart like a piece of gleaming jade, and quite naturally an outstanding example among women."

Unfortunately, no other information could be found on this Nun Ji, but from the evaluation she made of Xie Daoyun (Lady Wang) and Zhang Xuan's sister, it appears that she was a skilled artist of character analysis which was an important component of philosophical discourse of the time. The diction and allusion contained in her verbal evaluation also suggest that she was highly educated. Because men and women did not mix socially, the male scholars who were curious about the relative merit of the two famous ladies could only rely on Nun Ji as she was in a unique position of knowing both ladies intimately, as well as commanding the knowledge for such a task. She rose to the occasion and made a succinct and well-composed evaluation which must have

---

[27] *Ibid.*, j. 1, Biography 9.

[28] *Ibid.*, j. 1, Biography 12.

[29] *Ibid.*, j. 1, Biography 13.

[30] *Jin shu*, j. 66, p. 2517; *Shishuo xinyu jiaojian*, XIX, 30, p. 528.

been highly esteemed, otherwise it would not have been reported in both the *Jin shu* and *Shishuo xinyu.*

In short, the activities of scholarly nuns seem to have included the study of *sutras* and *vinayas,* teaching, debating and philosophical discussions, expounding the *sutras* and the writing of compositions. In a later generation, the nun Zhisheng even wrote a commentary to a *sutra.*[31]

Political influence: As in the West, members of the clergy often involved themselves in court politics and palace intrigues, Buddhist nuns at times were also involved. Nuns are known to have visited womenfolk in their homes, including those of the nobility and the scholar-official class, ostensibly to preach and give spiritual guidance. Initially the nuns gained admirers among the official class and nobility for their intellectual and religious accomplishments. With the exception of Jingjian, Daoxing and Daoyi, the biographies of all the other nuns either commented on, or related incidents which serve to indicate that, an important personage or personages showed respect and admiration for the nun concerned. The following table shows the kind of people with whom they were said to have been associated:

NAME OF NUN	PATRON AND STATUS OF PATRON
An Lingshou	Emperor Shi Hu
Zhixian	Emperor Fu Jian
Miaoxing	Governor of Hongnong
Minggan	He Chong (Prime Minister)*
Tanbei	Emperor Mu
	Empress He
Huizhan	He Chong (Prime Minister)*
Sengji	Emperor Kang
	Empress Chu
Daorong	Emperor Ming
	Emperor Jianwen
	Emperor Xiaowu
Lingzong	Emperor Xiaowu
Miaoyin	Emperor Xiaowu
	Sima Daozi (Prime Minister)* and
	Prince of Kuaiji

*He Chong and Sima Daozi did not have the official title of Prime Minister, but their positions were the equivalent.

Gradually the nuns became friends and confidantes of these rich and powerful people who would consult them on many matters, even matters of state. Daorong and Zhi Miaoyin perhaps represent the two stages of influence. Earlier we have related Daorong's alleged sainthood

---

[31] *Biqiuni zhuan*, j. 3, Biography 6.

and her magical powers. Under her influence, Emperor Jianwen transferred court patronage completely from Daoism to Buddhism. Hence her biography claims that because of her influence, Buddhism enjoyed a special place in the Jin Court henceforth.[32]

Daorong merely enjoyed the high esteem of the emperors Ming and Jianwen. Zhi Miaoyin went one step further to actually exert influence in matters of state on Emperor Xiaowu and probably also on his younger brother, Sima Daozi, into whose hands political power later fell. We have seen earlier that she often held philosophical discussions and wrote compositions together with the Emperor and Sima Daozi. Scholars and officials of lesser status naturally sought her company even more. The *Biqiuni zhuan* describes her influence as follows:

> In the tenth year of Taiyuan (385) the Grand Tutor built the Jianjing Convent for her and made her the abbess. Her disciples numbered more than one hundred. People of ability sought to become well known through her introduction, hence they gave endless donations and gifts. It became the richest convent in the capital. Nobles and commoners alike looked on her as their teacher. Every day there would be more than a hundred carriages outside her gate. When the Governor of Jingzhou, Wang Chen, died, Liezong (Emperor Xiaowu) intended to replace him with Wang Gong. At the time Huan Xuan was in Jiangling. He had been humiliated and oppressed by Chen. When he heard that Gong should go [to take Chen's place], and being always afraid of Gong, Xuan knew that Yin Zhongkan, who was Gong's disciple at the time, lacked in talent and would be easily controlled; hence he sent an emissary to obtain the Governorship for [Zhong]kan through the nun Miaoyin. Later Liezong asked Miaoyin, "The Governorship of Jingzhou has become vacant. According to public opinion, who should be Governor?" She replied, "I am a student of religion, I should not be concerned with the comments and discussions of the world. [But] I seem to have heard commentators everywhere say that there is no-one better than Yin Zhongkan, as he is a profound man with foresight. It is what Jingzhou needs." The Emperor agreed and replaced Chen with [Zhong]kan. Her power overruled the whole court, and she was regarded with awe by everyone both inside and outside the palace.[33]

Miaoyin's political activities can be corroborated in the official history *Jin shu*, where another incident of her attempting to interfere with court politics is found in two separate references.[34] One of these is quoted below:

> Guobao, [Fan] Ning's maternal nephew was Daozi's sycophant. Ning memorialized the Emperor to demote him. Guobao was frightened, he asked Yuan Yuezhi of Chen commandery to present a letter to Lady Chen, the Crown Prince's mother, through the nun Miaoyin, in which he said

---

[32] *Ibid.*, j. 1, Biography 10.

[33] *Ibid.*, j. 1, Biography 12.

[34] *Jin shu*, j. 64, p. 1734 and j. 75, p. 1971.

that Guobao was loyal and sensible, and should be befriended and trusted.[35]

From the above quotations, Miaoyin appears to have been very active in the political arena of the day. However, she must be considered an extreme example rather than the norm. Nevertheless, no matter what their political influence might have been, nuns of this period did not hold any official positions. This honour did not come until a later regime when Buddhism came almost to enjoy the position of a national religion. In the Southern Dynasty of Song, Emperor Ming appointed a nun to be the Director of *sangha* in the Capital Region,[36] an office responsible for exercising control over the *sangha*, as by that time the number of nuns had grown to a considerable size. In the same year, the emperor also appointed another nun to be *weina* of the Capital Region,[37] in charge of the routine of the convents. Both nuns, though, only had jurisdiction over the community of nuns.

Evangelical ability: In the biography of the first nun, Jingjian, we have a graphic description of the power of her preaching: "When she preached the *dharma*, it was like the wind over grass."[38] Another nun who devoted herself to preaching was Miaoxiang. From her biography we learn that "Often when she preached the law to convert people, she feared her listeners would not be firm in their aspiration, she sometimes broke down and cried while trying to convince them. Therefore those who received their first teaching from her all developed into successful converts."[39] Those who were ordained on account of An Lingshou were said to have numbered more than two hundred, but *Biqiuni zhuan* does not specify whether this number included those ordained as nuns only, so some of them might have been ordained as monks.

Management: As Buddhism established itself more and more firmly in China, the work of the *sangha* went beyond the spiritual needs of the people. As the size of monasteries and convents grew, the responsibility of their heads increased proportionally. The head of a large monastery or convent had to take care of the daily needs such as food, housing, clothing of a few hundred people, as well as the maintenance of buildings and images and carrying out restoration work. Moreover, the personnel side demanded considerable attention too, e.g. the distribution of work, the keeping of order, the meting out of rewards and punishments. Rapid expansion also called for the construction of new buildings for worship and housing. The convent—*si*—in those days consisted of a number of buildings for different

---

[35] *Ibid.*, j. 64, p. 1734.
[36] *Biqiuni zhuan*, j. 2, Biography 22.
[37] *Ibid.*
[38] *Ibid.*, j. 1, Biography 1.
[39] *Ibid.*, j. 1, Biography 4.

purposes.[40] The "audience hall" or Buddha hall was for placement of the images of Buddha and the bodhisattvas, hence it was a place of worship; but it was also used for meetings. The meditation hall or rooms were usually located a short way from the main hall in a quieter part of the convent; besides the obvious purpose of meditation, smaller lectures were also held in them. Most lectures, though, were held in lecture halls, and some of them were open to the public. The "*sutra hall*" was used to house copies of *sutras* and *vinayas*, and perhaps it also served as a reading room. The living quarters were in most cases separate units or rooms. With residents numbering from more than one hundred to several hundreds, as mentioned in the *Biqiuni zhuan*, the number of units to be provided was in itself a formidable task. The building of cult objects such as *stupas* and the making of images out of various materials (such as wood, stone and bronze with gold plating)— sometimes of enormous size—also demanded time and money. The source of a convent's income was mainly donations, hence it was important to be on good terms with rich and powerful believers and to understand the intricacies of soliciting funds from them. The biographies of both Zhixian and Sengji record that they managed convents of more than one hundred people with outstanding success. Sengji is especially praised as a wise administrator, as seen in our earlier discussion concerning the nuns' administrative talents. It is recorded in An Lingshou's biography that she had built five or six convents. In Tanbei's biography, her disciple Tanluo was said to have built a four-storey *stupa*, a lecture hall and living quarters. In a later period, a nun seems to have specialized in building images and adopted it as her life-long vocation. She did not just build them for her own convent, but for many other temples and monasteries as well.[41] These nuns displayed great capability in the planning and execution of such ambitious building programmes.

Charity work: In the Jin period only one of the thirteen nuns is recorded as having helped and cared for the sick and the poor, though it is difficult to imagine that she was the only one to do work of this nature. In this respect we should perhaps keep in mind that the author of these biographies was male, and a scholarly type. From his unavoidably patriarchal and Confucian view, what was worthy of recording might have centred upon Buddhist learning and teaching, hence although many nuns may have devoted themselves to charity work, he may not have found this aspect of particular importance. For example, in Jingjian's biography, it was said that even though she received numerous donations from the faithful, she distributed them immediately. It is probable that some of these donations would have gone to help the poor.

---

[40] Cissell, *op. cit.*, pp. 79-84.
[41] *Biqiuni zhuan*, j. 2, Biography 4.

61

The following passage in the biography of Lingzong provides us with some information of her charity work:

> Later, among the common people many were sick and poverty-stricken. After spending all her own money to help them, Lingzong went out begging in the world, even to distant and remote places. She gave money according to need. Many benefited from her charity or were saved by it. As a result of starvation and hard work, she looked withered and exhausted. [42]

Her story is reminiscent of that of some Catholic nuns of the West. One significant difference is that no reference is made to any nursing activity by her or any other Chinese nun. They seem to have had little to do with the medical profession.

The achievement of the early Chinese nuns is impressive. These pioneers succeeded in establishing models which nuns of the centuries following would emulate. In some cases even higher levels of achievement were attained by later nuns. For example, in the field of scholarship, it was not until the next period—the Southern and Northern Dynasties—that a nun first wrote a commentary to a *sutra*. It was also in the next period that two nuns were named government officials by imperial decree. There are also some aspects of achievement which were not pioneered in this period—asceticism, missionary work and the art of meditation—to name a few. The *Biqiuni zhuan* shows that they either began or reached their peak of achievement during the Southern and Northern Dynasties.

In conclusion, I would like to offer a few thoughts concerning the social ramifications of the emergence of Buddhist nuns in China. Firstly, the convents opened up new avenues of vocation for women. Judging from the information provided by the *Biqiuni zhuan*, there were many accomplished women among the earliest nuns. In ancient China, the only role for a woman was that of a wife and mother. Life was probably simpler if a woman was born in a poor family because she would need all her wits to scratch out an existence for herself and her family. Women born into better families were normally freed from the drudgery of production and housework; they were also often taught the basics in reading and writing, but were discouraged from doing anything with their learning except writing ephemeral poetry and prose. As a result, some of the women of this class who were born with talent were not satisfied with the role they were assigned to play, and preferred an alternative role. Heretofore, women of talent and aspiration were not offered any alternatives, therefore they often felt a great sense of frustration. This situation was often further aggravated by an unsatisfactory marriage in which the husband was inferior or

---

[42] *Ibid.*, j. 1, Biography 11.

uncaring.[43] Hence the convent provided an attractive alternative to Chinese women who, for whatever reason, wished to escape the traditional pattern of marriage and domestic life. One such motive could have been to end an unsatisfactory marriage, for in ancient China a man could divorce his wife by using one of the seven reasons given in the law; but there was no such provision in the law for women and therefore it was very difficult for a woman to divorce her husband. Another was that widows could escape having a second marriage arranged by relatives through entering a convent. For women with talent and aspiration, the convent offered an opportunity to further develop their intellect. Women of rich or middle-class families who had been taught to read and write would have welcomed the chance to put their talent and learning to some use. Girls from poor families who did not have the opportunity to learn at all would have welcomed the facilities provided by a convent. Nuns could also do a variety of work otherwise not available to them, such as research on Buddhist texts, teaching, preaching, administration, building and construction. In addition, nuns enjoyed much more freedom of movement than women living at home. They could travel to other cities in order to study under famous masters without worrying about public opinion or travel expenses, as they normally begged on the way or stayed at Buddhist establishments which were obliged to provide them with free lodging and vegetarian food. Also there seem to have been no taboos on associating with male *sangha* and lay members in such activities as the borrowing of *sutras* and *vinaya* texts, and in attending lectures and even participating in philosophical discussions in mixed company.

Secondly, it increased the power of women to influence society. Famous nuns were known to have befriended empresses and emperors, not to mention lesser dignitaries. Some among them even acted as consultants to these important people, and so could influence the appointment of officials and wield great power in politics. We have seen that one nun was reputed to have caused the Jin court to change its patronage from Daoism to Buddhism, and another to have caused the emperor to change his mind about the appointment of a governor. The only other way for a woman to have the same kind of influence was to be married to the emperor. Sometimes nuns abused the confidence and trust placed in them by meddling in the affairs of state, as exemplified by Miaoyin's story quoted earlier. In later years unscrupulous elements infiltrated the ranks of the nuns and even involved themselves in witchcraft and bloody palace intrigues.[44]

---

[43] A typical example of this type is Xie Daoyun. See *Jin shu*, j. 96, p. 2516.

[44] *Song shu*, j. 99, p. 2425. Though the shamaness Yan Daoyu, who played an important role in the bloody coup of Heir-Apparent Shao, was not a nun, she disguised herself as one and was referred to by others as a nun.

Thirdly, the appearance of nuns increased women's contacts with the outside world. Usually women from good families were not able to go out freely, and thus they had very little contact with the outside world. Nuns visited the women in their homes and because they themselves could travel and therefore knew all the latest news and gossip of the nation, they broadened the knowledge and vision of women in general. Nuns also served as teachers to the women at home and probably contributed to increasing the literacy of Chinese women. On the negative side, Buddhist nuns, together with their Daoist counterparts, were often portrayed as instigators or at least ready accessories to women who wished to get rid of a relative or rival by procuring poison or other instruments of murder. They may well have also been responsible for a great deal of malicious gossip as they travelled from door to door.

In short, the appearance of nuns in Chinese society made a profound impression on the life of women in medieval China. While it did not actually make life easier for all women, it nevertheless enabled some of them to live a freer and fuller life on the fringes of Chinese culture.

Where Are the Heroines of the Long March Now?
A Survey of Their Lives and Work After 1949

The Long March of the Chinese Communist Army (CCP) is regarded with awe and adoration in China, sometimes to religious proportions, and has captured the imagination of many people in the West. Among the numerous accounts written about them are the works of Edgar and Helen Snow, Agnes Smedley and more recently, Salisbury's book, *The Long March: the Untold Story*,[1] all of which have devoted some attention to the indomitable women who endured far more hardships than their male counterparts on the Long March. Salisbury has even devoted a whole chapter of his book to these women.

Yet after so much anguish, what have they received in return? It is probably true that when these young women and girls undertook the Long March, at least some of them did it for the sake of an ideal, and they did not think of any future rewards. But after 1949, when the veterans of the Long March were rewarded with various favourable positions in the newly formed nation, it is of interest to see if the women enjoyed similar privileges. It is the purpose of this paper to find out, as far as the information available allows, how the women who took part in the Long March fared after the establishment of the People's Republic of China.

First of all, it is necessary to find out how many women actually took part in the Long March and who they were. However, it is extremely difficult to reach an accurate figure. There were women in the First, Second, Fourth Front Armies and the Twenty-Fifth Army.[2] Most sources state that thirty women started out from Ruijin (Jiangxi province) with the First Front Army. A list of the thirty women is found in a thin volume on the Long March published in Shanghai in 1938.[3] The names in this list are full of errors, perhaps intentional, to protect the relatives of these women still living in the Guomindang controlled areas. I have identified all thirty of these women—who are listed below—except for one, Li Xiaojiang. This name does not appear in any of the later publications. However, a Li Guiying, who definitely left with the thirty from Jiangxi[4] is not in this list. It is therefore likely that Li Xiaojiang was in fact Li Guiying, as many communists were known to have had aliases in those days.

---

[1] For example: Edgar Snow, *Red Star Over China*; Helen Foster Snow, *Chinese Communists: Sketches and Autobiographies of the Old Guards*; Agnes Smedley, *The Great Road*, and Harrison E. Salisbury, *The Long March: The Untold Story*.

[2] Liaowang Bianjibu (ed.), *Hongjun nüyingxiong zhuan*, p. 2.

[3] Zhu Lifu, *Erwan wuqian li changzheng ji*, pp. 67-8.

[4] *Ibid.*, p. 157.

Liu Ying (wife of Lo Fu, b. 1912)
Chen Qing (wife of Deng Fa, more commonly known as Chen Huiqing, 1909-1983)
Liu Qunxian (wife of Bo Gu, 1907-?1941)
Wei Gongzhi (wife of Ye Jianying, 1903-1973)
Wei Xiuying (b. 1910)
Li Bozhao (wife of Yang Shangkun, 1911-1985)
Cai Chang (wife of Li Fuchun, 1900-1990)
Li Jianzhen (b. 1906)
Jin Weiying (first wife of Deng Xiaoping, Li Weihan's wife during the Long March, 1904-?1941)
He Zhijian (more commonly known as He Zizhen, wife of Mao Zedong, 1910-1984)
Liao Shiguang (more commonly known as Liao Siguang, b. 1911)
Qian Xijun (Mao Zemin's wife, b. 1905)
Han Shiying (probably Kan Siying, alias Gan Tang, 1910-1971)
Deng Yingchao (wife of Zhou Enlai, 1904-1992)
Zhou Yuehua (1904-1977)
Liao Yuehua (probably Xiao Yuehua, 1915-1983)
A Xiang (later identified as Xie Fei, former wife of Liu Shaoqi, b. 1913)
Wu Hulian (probably Wu Fulian, 1912-1937)
Wang Qianyuan (probably Wang Quanyuan, b. 1913)
Wu Zhonglian (1908-1967)
Deng Liujin (b. 1912)
Xie Xiaomei (b. 1913)
Zhong Yulin (probably Zhong Yuelin, b. 1915)
Liu Caixiang (probably Liu Caixia, 1915-1980)
Zheng Yu (probably Zeng Yu, 1908-?1941)
Yang Houzeng (probably Yang Houzhen, 1908-1977)
Li Xiaojiang (? alias Li Guiying, b. 1912)
Li Jianhua (b. 1915)
Kang Keqing (wife of Zhu De, b. 1910)
Qiu Yihan (1907-1956)

This list above gives cadres only. According to Helen Foster Snow, twenty other women also marched with them.[5] These included nurses, and orderlies,[6] perhaps even a sewing team to keep the army supplied

[5] H. F. Snow, *op. cit.*, p. 245.
[6] Salisbury, *op. cit.*, p. 79.

A photograph of the Long March women taken during a reunion in 1949.

with clothes and shoes.[7] The number who joined from the various other revolutionary bases is even harder to estimate. For example, in connection with the Fourth Front Army, one reads about such disparate groups as the Women's Independent Division, Regiment and Battalion, Women's Vanguard Regiment of the West Route Army, Women's Engineer Battalion, Women's Attachment. In the same Army there were also nurses in the General Hospital of the Army, and actresses, singers and dancers in the New Troupe. Commanded by Zhang Qinqiu, the Women's Independent Division (later Regiment) alone had about two thousand women. The Women's Vanguard Regiment was said to have had an additional one thousand three hundred members or so under the command of Wang Quanyuan. Most of the women in these two outfits died or were taken prisoners in Gansu in the bloodiest battles ever fought by the Red Army and were never heard of again.[8]

The CCP has been extremely reluctant to publish biographical information concerning its members, even more so regarding the women members, some of whom are the wives of party leaders. However since the late seventies, there has been a significant change, and a proliferation of biographical material is being written, compiled and published. Without this change, a paper such as this one could never have been written. What I find particularly helpful are details included in two very useful monographs: Guo Chen's *Jinguo liezhuan* is on the experience of the thirty women cadres who started from Jiangxi and what is known about their later life,[9] while Dong Hanhe's *Xilujun nüzhanshi mengnan ji* is an attempt to reconstruct the story of women in the Western Route Army which was devastated by the Cavalry of the Ma clan of Gansu.[10]

From the various sources I have collected the names of fifty-eight women about whom enough material is provided to make a meaningful

---

[7] In Lin Yueqin's biography in Liaowang Bianjibu (ed.), *Hongjun nüyingxiong zhuan* (p. 26) she is said to have headed a Women's Engineer Battalion of the Fourth Front Army which was responsible for the manufacture of uniforms and straw hats. A similar outfit might have existed in the First Front Army.

[8] *Zhonggong dangshi renwu zhuan*, Vol. 17, pp. 247-55 and Liaowang Bianjibu (ed.), *Hongjun nüyingxiong zhuan*, pp. 199-205. For an attempt to recreate the massacre the women of the West Route Army experienced, see Dong Hanhe, *Xilujun nüzhanshi mengnan ji*.

[9] Guo Chen, *Jinguo liezhuan: hong yifangmian jun sanshi wei changzheng nü Hongjun shengping shiji.*

[10] Dong Hanhe, *op. cit.*

study.[11] Two other women, Zeng Xianzhi and Chen Shaomin, are also said to have completed the Long March in some sources,[12] but this information is not confirmed by recent Chinese publications. Of the fifty-eight women in our study, thirty were with the First Front Army who had started out from Jiangxi with Mao Zedong, Zhu De and Zhou Enlai; twenty-one started from Sichuan with Zhang Guotao; six with the Second Front Army from Hunan with He Long and Xiao Ke, and one with the Twenty-fifth Army from Hubei with Xu Haidong.

Personal Background

First of all, in order to gain better insight into the women who embarked on this odyssey, I shall attempt to take a look at the background of the fifty-eight in our study.

Their birth dates range from 1900 to 1923. The oldest of them is Cai Chang, one of the earliest members of the CCP and famous worker on women issues, who was born in 1900, and Chen Zongying, wife of Ren Bishi, born in 1902. These women were in their early thirties at the time of the Long March and were "old" compared with the majority of their comrades. Cai was generally referred to as "Big Sister" by everyone. The youngest are two nurses in the Fourth Front Army named Shi Qunying, born in 1922, and Ma Yixiang, born in 1923, who were among those "red little devils" mentioned in the works of Edgar Snow, Nym Wales (i.e., Helen Snow) and Rewi Alley. They were only eleven and twelve when they started on the Long March. If we look at the distribution according to birth date in Table I, we will find that the majority of them were born between 1910 and 1919. This group consisted of thirty-one women.

---

[11] This is a list of their names:
Cai Chang, Chen Huiqing, Chen Luoying, Chen Zhenren, Chen Zongying, Dai Juemin, Deng Liujin, Deng Yingchao, Gan Tang (also known as Kan Siying), Guo Changchun, He Lianzhi, He Zizhen, Jian Xianfo, Jian Xianren, Jin Weiying, Kang Keqing, Li Bozhao, Li Guiying, Li Jian, Li Jianhua, Li Jianzhen, Li Kaifang, Li Zhen, Liao Siguang, Lin Jiang, Lin Yueqin, Liu Caixia, Liu Jian, Liu Liqing, Liu Qunxian, Liu Ying, Ma Yixiang, Qian Xijun, Qiu Yihan, Quan Weihua, Shi Qunying, Wang Dingguo, Wang Quanyuan, Wang Ronghua, Wang Zenan, Wei Gongzhi, Wei Xiuying, Wu Chaoxiang, Wu Fulian, Wu Shunying, Wu Zhonglian, Xiao Yuehua, Xie Fei, Xie Xiaomei, Yang Houzhen, Yang Lei, Yang Wenju, Zeng Yu, Zhang Mingxiu, Zhang Ping (Zhang Xianxiu), Zhang Qinqiu, Zhong Yuelin, Zhou Yuehua.
[12] *Zhonggong renming lu.*

TABLE I
DISTRIBUTION OF WOMEN MARCHERS BY BIRTH DATE

YEAR OF BIRTH		NUMBER
1900-1904		7
1905-1909		12
1910-1914		16
1915-1919		19
1920-1924		4
	Total	58

An analysis of the birth places of the women marchers reveals that they came from a wide variety of provinces, though as one would expect, Jiangxi and Sichuan—where the largest red bases were established—both claim a large proportion. However, the number who came from Hunan, where only a small base was established by He Long, exceeds Jiangxi. That, of course, is because many of the earliest communists were Mao Zedong's friends and associates from Hunan. Except for four women from Jiangsu and Zhejiang, all were from provinces where red bases had been established. The four exceptions were connected to the labour movement in or around Shanghai in the 1920s. Table II shows the distribution of the women marchers according to their birth place. Interestingly, not all of the women were of Han origin. Among the 58 studied, two were from minority groups: one Moslem and one of Tujia origin.

TABLE II
DISTRIBUTION OF WOMEN MARCHERS BY BIRTH PLACE

BIRTH PLACE		NUMBER
Anhui		2
Fujian		3
Guangdong		5
Henan		3
Hubei		2
Hunan		11
Jiangsu		1
Jiangxi		9
Shaanxi		1
Sichuan		18
Zhejiang		3
	Total	58

As can be surmised, the majority of the women came from very poor families and many were sold or given away as *tongyangxi* or child-wives. (These were girls from poor families which could not support them so they were sent to live with the family of their prospective husbands long before marrying age. Usually they were ill-treated and used as a source of slave labour. However, some of the women say they did not suffer maltreatment. In some cases, the boy they were intended to marry died young, and they were raised as adopted daughters.) My sources do not always give information concerning family background, but it is possible to infer this through other details provided, for example, if the woman had had some schooling, which suggests that she did not come from a poor peasant family. She could have come either from a middle class or an intelligentsia family. For lack of a term which can encompass a variety of situations, such as small landowners, small business proprietors, shop assistants, teachers, etc., I have used the rather vague term of "middle class". I have tried to distinguish categories mainly on the basis of poor peasant backgrounds or middle class backgrounds. A further two categories are included because explicit information is available. The "scholar-official" category refers to families descended from or still had close relatives who had served in the Qing or Republican government. The "revolutionary" category refers to those families in which other members had become communist activists before the woman herself. Table III shows that twenty-eight women were from a poor peasant background, seventeen of whom said they had been child-wives. From the fifteen who had not come from poor peasant families, one had been a child-wife.

TABLE III
FAMILY BACKGROUND

TYPE	NUMBER
Poor peasant background	34
Middle class background	18
Scholar-official background	3
Revolutionary background	3
Total	58

The educational level of our protagonists is also of special interest, because all of them, at one time or another, were or still are cadres with different degrees of responsibility. Table IV represents the result of my analysis of their educational level before the Long March. It must be noted that the levels mentioned in the table merely show that they had attended schools of that level, but by no means signify that they had successfully completed that level. It should be noted that the people whose educational level is unknown most probably had not received much formal education. Classes for the learning of Chinese characters in the cadre schools and party schools before the Long March, as well as the *shiziban*, cannot really be classified as formal education. One woman said that only the text of the current policy documents was studied in such classes. The classes usually lasted from a few weeks to a few months. Consequently, we can say that twenty-five of the women received some sort of formal education, while thirty-three most probably had not. Out of those who went abroad to study, Cai Chang was the only one who did not go to the Soviet Union; she was in the Work-Study Programme which helped students to study in France. Again, not everyone who went abroad finished a formal programme of study there.

TABLE IV
EDUCATION LEVEL BEFORE THE LONG MARCH

TYPE OF SCHOOL		NUMBER
Formal:		
Primary		9
High school		2
Normal school		5
Military school		2
Studied abroad		7
	Total	25
Informal or other:		
Soviet area party and cadre schools		10
Classes for learning characters		1
Self-study		1
Not ascertained		21
	Total	33

After the Long March, those who reached Yan'an were usually rewarded with an opportunity to study at one or more of the schools and universities in Northern Shaanxi. Some of the women also furthered their studies in a technical subject, such as medicine, wireless operation, etc. After 1949, a few took time off to study at regular universities and obtained academic degrees. Table V shows the number of people who took advantage of the opportunity of further study and the various kinds of ways they chose to do it. Not all women continued their education. On the other hand, some of them attended more than one institution, for example, many attended two or more of the following: the Yan'an Anti-Japanese Military and Political University, the Central Party School, and the the Marxist-Leninist Academy. Hence no attempt has been made to give a total.

TABLE V
FURTHER EDUCATION AFTER THE LONG MARCH

TYPE OF EDUCATION	NUMBER
Yan'an Anti-Japanese Military and Political University	10
Central Party School and its branches	20
Yan'an Marxist-Leninist Academy	3
Yan'an Medical University	1
Red Army Medical College	2
Central Cadre School	1
Regional party schools	3
Radio operation	1
Preparatory school for university	1
Regular universities	3
Institutions in USSR	2
Self-study with help of others	1
No schooling mentioned	8
Died before reaching Yan'an	1

The educational institutions in Yan'an tended to be under less pressure to push students through due to the urgent need of trained workers—which was the case in the soviet bases—and were able to devote time to a comparatively more thorough education. Conditions were still extremely difficult. Due to air raids, some classes had to be held in mountain gullies in the open. Writing materials such as pencils and paper were also difficult to obtain. As a result of further education after the Long March, it is possible that none of the women remained illiterate. At the other end of the scale, three women graduated from universities and one of them qualified as a doctor. One interesting thing about this only doctor of the group, Shi Qunying, is that after becoming a doctor and rising to the position of Deputy Director of the Navy Hospital in Nanjing, she entered the Education Department of Beijing Normal University and re-trained as a teacher. Then she became the Deputy Mistress of a navy primary school. Compared to those who had studied in the USSR, she probably achieved a great deal more, because in Russia, the institutions at which most Chinese students studied were usually created for students from Asian countries only, and were below the standard of a university.

Many of the women went on the Long March because they were the wives of CCP leaders or high level army commanders. Some married during or soon after reaching Yan'an. It is therefore of interest to investigate their marriage status and partners. Twenty-six women married before the start of the March, two were married during it, and eighteen were married afterwards. One died without ever marrying. We have no information concerning the marriage status of the remaining eleven women. Of the married women, four of them married more than once. Zhang Qinqiu and Li Guiying married three times. There had been one case of divorce before the Long March, i.e., the divorce of Jin Weiying and Deng Xiaoping (after which Jin married Li Weihan, one of the Bolsheviks in power before the Long March). After the end of the March, six more divorces occurred, among them the best known being the divorce of He Zizhen and Mao Zedong. The others are those between

Xiao Yuehua and Otto Braun (Li De)
Jin Weiying and Li Weihan
Liu Qunxian and Bo Gu[13]
Xie Fei And Liu Shaoqi
Jian Xianren and He Long

The majority of the spouses of the forty-six women whose marital status is known were among the top leaders, numbering twenty-three altogether; sixteen of them were high level cadres of the party, the government and the military, and eleven were middle and lower level ones. Only one was a professional man: Dr Norman Fu (Nelson Fu in some sources) or Fu Lianzhang who accompanied the Long March and married one of his nurses. The top group of leaders includes Mao Zedong, Liu Shaoqi, Zhou Enlai, Zhu De, Mao Zemin, Li Fuchun, Luo Fu (Zhang Wentian), Bo Gu, Li De, Chen Changhao, Ren Bishi and He Long.

Except for Xiao Yuehua, all women had become members of the CCP or its Youth League before embarking on the Long March. Most of the Youth League members received party membership after they arrived in the north of Shaanxi in 1936 or 1937 with the exception of Li Jian, who became a member during the Long March. A very special case is that of Wei Gongzhi. Wei had joined the CCP in 1926, but was expelled as a Trotskyite in 1931. It was not until after she had completed the Long March that she was reinstated.

In order to provide some reference to their work after 1949, it is necessary to find out what kind of work the women were doing before and during the Long March. Table VI shows the position of the women before and during the Long March. A brief explanation is perhaps necessary in regard to the classification.

---

[13] H. F. Snow, *op. cit.*, p. 318; Donald Klein and Anne Clark (eds), *Biographic Dictionary of Chinese Communism, 1921-1965*, p. 386.

Top leadership	members of the CCP Central Committee
	members of the central government and its ministers and deputy ministers
High level cadres	central government officials below ministerial level
	leadership of mass organizations (e.g., Women's Federation, The Trade Union)
	party secretaries of provincial or regional level
	leadership of military regions
Middle and lower level cadres	all other bureaucrats of the party, the government and the military
Logistics, medical and entertainment workers	Those whose work involved transportation, finding food and water, nursing, organizing and actually taking part in entertainment programmes

Transportation usually means carrying grain or the sick and wounded on their backs. Entertainment refers to the kind of message-laden performance of song, dance and simple dramatic presentation devoted to the required topic for the propaganda of the day. The purpose of such entertainment was expressly to educate the people of the area in political ideology and to boost the morale of the soldiers. It can be seen quite clearly that many middle and low level women cadres before the Long March were transferred to the "logistics, medical and entertainment workers" category due to the urgent need during the Long March for women to shoulder such responsibilities in order to free men for fighting. Besides, the Red Army experienced great difficulty in the recruiting of paid carriers, and the desertion rate of those recruited was also very high.[14]

---

[14] Liaowang Bianjibu, *op. cit.*, p. 47 and Salisbury, *op. cit.*, p. 88.

TABLE VI
POSITION OF WOMEN BEFORE AND DURING
THE LONG MARCH

POSITION	BEFORE	DURING
Top leadership	4	2
High level cadres	3	4
Middle and low level cadres	45	24
Logistics, medical and entertainment workers	6	25
No work	0	3
Total	58	58

For most of the women the Long March took almost exactly a year. They suffered fatigue, hunger, illness, inclement weather, treacherous roads, not to mention the anguish of giving birth while fighting and fleeing from the enemy, and worst of all, having to leave the new born baby behind without knowing if it would ever be found again. In fact, most were never found. He Zizhen, Mao's wife, and several like her, had to give up more than one baby in her lifetime.

The First Quarter of a Century

When the PRC was established in 1949, a new administration needed to be organized and thousands of positions needed to be filled by reliable, long-serving party members. At the same time, the party probably also felt that its faithful should be suitably rewarded. Male veterans of the Long March were given responsible positions. Whether female veterans enjoyed the same kind of privilege is one of the points which this investigation seeks to clarify.

By 1949 five of the women who went on the Long March had died. They were Zeng Yu, Jin Weiying, Liu Qunxian, Wu Fulian and Li Jianhua. Before the outbreak of the Cultural Revolution, one more was added to the list: Qiu Yihan died in 1956 of illness. Jin was a member of the Executive Committee of the Central Soviet Government before the Long March. She divorced Deng Xiaoping before the Long March to marry Li Weihan, one of the Bolsheviks who were in power at the time.[15] One source said she died in 1940, another said 1941, of illness, in the USSR where she had undergone some treatment.[16] The second was Liu Qunxian, a union leader of Wuxi in the 1920s and the wife of Bo Gu, who was the leader of the Bolsheviks. For a month during the Long March she was in charge of a women's battalion, but this

---

[15] Salisbury, *op. cit.*, p. 141.
[16] *Huaxia funü mingren cidian*, p. 691, and Qiu Zhizhuo, *Zhonggong dangshi renminglu*, p. 306.

battalion was dispersed after Zunyi, presumably because Bo Gu lost power to Mao at the Zunyi Conference. One source said she died in 1940 while receiving treatment in the USSR, another said that she died in a German air-raid in 1941;[17] she is also said to have been divorced by Bo Gu before that.[18] Whether it was purely coincidental that the wives of two important Bolsheviks died about the same time in the USSR is a matter for speculation. Wu Fulian was one of the thirty women who started with the First Front Army from Jiangxi, but she was re-assigned to the Fourth Front Army and later was the Political Commissar for the Women's Vanguard Regiment of the West Route Army which perished in Gansu, as mentioned above. She was taken prisoner and died of injuries and sickness in 1937.[19] The two who were presumed to have died are Zeng Yu and Li Jianhua: Zeng worked in the New Fourth Army after the Long March, and disappeared in 1941 on her way back from Hunan where she had taken her child to be cared for by relatives.[20] With regard to Li Jianhua, who was also presumed to have died before 1949, the last information we have on her is that she had helped Kang Keqing to transmit Zhu De's directive to other members of the First Front Army assigned to the Fourth Front army of Zhang Guotao, and "saw the successful rendezvous of the First and the Fourth Front Army in 1936."[21]

Three of the women—Cai Chang, Zhang Qinqiu and Deng Yingchao—were among the top leadership in 1949. All three were elected to the Presidium in September that year to plan the formation of the new Republic, as well as to the Central People's Government. Cai Chang had been a member and Deng an alternate member of the CCP Central Committee since 1945. In 1949 Zhang Qinqiu was appointed Vice-Minister of the Textile Industry of the newly formed People's Republic. She was the only Communist woman to attain such high rank in the new regime. (Song Qingling who was given the title of Vice-President of the state was not from the ranks of the Communist Party.) Deng Yingchao was standing member of the Chinese People's Political Consultative Conference, and she and Cai Chang were on the Standing Committee of the People's Assembly from its beginning in 1954. Cai Chang was President of the All-China Federation of Democratic Women, the highest women's organization of the whole nation, while Deng was its Vice-President and Zhang was on both its standing and executive committees.

The majority of the women became officials of the party, the government or the military. Five of them were among the high level cadres and thirty-two fell into the group of middle and lower level

---

[17] *Huaxia funü mingren cidian*, p. 281; Qiu, *op. cit.*, p. 125.
[18] H. F. Snow, *op. cit.*, p. 318.
[19] Guo, *op. cit.*, p. 193.
[20] *Ibid*, p. 81.
[21] *Ibid*, p. 179.

cadres. (The criteria of classification are the same as those used above.) It is interesting to note that some women decided on a career change at this juncture. A few of the women turned to professional work. Li Bozhao became a professional dramatist and was appointed Director of the People's Art Theatre of Beijing, and at the same time held the post of Vice-President of the Central Academy of Drama. She had studied literature and drama in the Soviet Union before the Long March, and all through the Long March was responsible for creating plays and other kinds of entertainment to lift the morale of the soldiers and raise the political awareness of both the army and the people. She was also the former wife of Yang Shangkun, the veteran general whose name is associated with the military suppression of students in Tiananmen on 4 June 1989.

Chen Zhenren, wife of Dr Norman Fu, worked as a pharmacist after the Long March, and in 1948 when Beijing was liberated, as the Deputy Head of the Pharmaceutical Supply Section of the newly established Health Department of the Military Commission, she went to Beijing to take over the health work of that city. In 1950 she was responsible for organizing the Second All-Military Pharmaceutical Supply Workshop in which the experiences of the war years were summarized and future policies formulated.

Shi Qunying, the second youngest member of our group, was trained in Yan'an as a doctor. In 1949 she headed a clinic in the North-China Military Region. Before 1954 she was promoted to Deputy Director of the Navy Hospital in Nanjing. A similar example is Yang Lei, who had been trained in a series of army medical schools and worked as a doctor and hospital administrator after 1949.

Three of the women had no work in 1949. In the case of Wei Gongzhi, it was because of prolonged illness. In the case of Lin Yueqin, it was because she was asked to devote her time exclusively to the care of her sick husband, Director of the General Political Department, Marshal Luo Ronghuan. It is far more complicated in the case of Wang Quanyuan. Wang was the commander of the Women's Vanguard Regiment of the West Route Army of Zhang Guotao. This army was decimated by the Cavalry of the Ma clan from Gansu, and Wang was captured along with many of the comrades of her Regiment. She was given by Ma Bufang, the commander of the Ma Cavalry, to a subordinate as a concubine. According to her biography,[22] she resisted and was beaten until half-dead, after which the officer was called away. With the help of a maidservant she recovered and, after two years, escaped. When she showed up at the Office of the Eighth Route Army in Lanzhou, she was turned away as a traitor. She begged her way back to her native province of Jiangxi. Though she is said to have rejoined

---

[22] Liaowang Bianjibu, *op. cit.*, pp. 201-5. Her story was corroborated by confessions made by a former officer of the Ma Cavalry in 1957 found by Dong Hanhe. See Dong, *op. cit.*, p. 56.

"revolutionary work" in 1949, she was not given a position until 1962 when Kang Keqing visited her in Jiangxi and demanded that she be given a position.[23] I have not been able to find out whether Xiao Yuehua, Otto Braun's wife, was assigned any work in 1949.

He Lianzhi, Dong Biwu's wife, who commanded a company of nurses during the Long March, carrying the wounded on their backs and caring for them, was a wife and mother in Yan'an, and after 1949 she was made Dong's personal secretary.

TABLE VII
POSITIONS HELD BY THE WOMEN IN 1949 AND
UP TO THE CULTURAL REVOLUTION

POSITION	1949	UP TO CULTURAL REVOLUTION
Top leadership	3	4
High level	5	10
Middle and low level	37	28
Professional	4	4
No work	3	5
Retired	0	1
Dead	5	6
Unknown	1	0
Total	58	58

From the above table we can see that from 1949 to the eve of the Cultural Revolution one more woman, Li Jianzhen, had advanced to the top leadership, and five more had advanced to high level cadres. Until the Cultural Revolution, the number of women who had no work increased from three to five. Wang Quanyuan, who had no work in the previous period, was given a "middle and low level" position. Lin Yueqin, who had to take care of her sick husband, had to become the Deputy Office Manager of his General Political Department to assist him in discharging his duties. When he died in 1963 she was given the rank of senior colonel. Xiao Yuehua, whose work status is unknown, was given a position, but retired the next year. He Zizhen, Mao's former wife, became ill, and Wei Gongzhi continued to be ill; both did not work. Three women lost their positions for political reasons: Xie Fei was called a "typical rightist" and a "Peng Dehuai style personage" in the anti-rightist movement of 1959. Liu Ying and Li Jian were both dismissed because their husbands, Zhang Wentian and Hou Zheng respectively, were labelled as rightists.

---

[23] Liaowang Bianjibu, pp. 205-6.

The number of deceased women Long Marchers increased by one to six. The number of women in professions remained four.

The Cultural Revolution

The Cultural Revolution brought calamity to many of the women in our study. Since both Jiang Qing and Ye Qun, the two top women of this period, did not participate in the Long March, they regarded the women veterans with animosity. Although the positions of two of the leading veterans, Cai Chang and Deng Yingchao, remained unchanged on the surface, their lives were made quite miserable. Cai Chang was called "mistress of the February countercurrent"—referring to a meeting in February 1967 in which the old guard, including her husband Li Fuchun, tried to turn the tide of the Cultural Revolution. Deng Yingchao was not attacked personally, but she had to watch helplessly as her husband Zhou Enlai was being humiliated while he was slowly dying of cancer and overwork. Her personal life was also severely restricted. Because of the precarious situation she and her husband were in, she saw no visitors, answered no mail and visited no-one.[24]

Seventeen women remained as middle and low level cadres without apparently being affected by the Cultural Revolution. For another six of the women, it is not known how the Cultural Revolution affected them. They were mostly from the middle and low level group, so presumably they were left unharmed due to their unimportance.

Nine women suffered moderate persecution during the Cultural Revolution: Chen Zhenren, Li Jianzhen, Li Zhen, Liao Siguang, Lin Jiang, Lin Yueqin, Wang Dinguo, Yang Wenju and Xie Xiaomei. Some, like Li Zhen and Liao Siguang, were imprisoned and interrogated; others, like Chen Zhenren, Xie Xiaomei and Lin Yueqin, were exiled to hard labour in the countryside. Li Zhen simply dissappeared. Nine suffered worse fates and were criticized and subjected to "struggle" sessions: Kang Keqing, Liu Ying, Li Bozhao, Zhong Yuelin, Li Guiying, Ma Yixiang, Liu Jian, Gan Tang and Xie Fei. Kang Keqing was persecuted for no other reason than the fact that her fate was bound up with that of her husband Zhu De. Zhu De was attacked in a big poster which called him a "black general" and charged with "shamelessly" claiming to be a founder of the Red Army.[25] Their house was ransacked by Red Guards and Kang Keqing was paraded in the streets. Zhu died a few months before Zhou Enlai and Mao Zedong, in the last moments of the Cultural Revolution. Zhang Qinqiu was persecuted to death in 1968, and Wei Gongzhi, Wu Zhonglian and Gan Tang died of natural causes, making the number of deceased a total of nine. He Zizhen and Li Jian were not allocated work.

---

[24] Fang Jucheng and Fang Guinong, *Zhou Enlai: A Profile by Percy Jucheng Fang and Lucy Guinong J. Fang*, p. 205, note 15.
[25] Salisbury, *op. cit.*, p. 336.

TABLE VIII
SITUATION OF WOMEN DURING THE CULTURAL
REVOLUTION 1966-1976

SITUATION	NUMBER
Not apparently affected	17
No work	2
Already retired	3
Already dead	9
Moderately persecuted	9
Severely persecuted	9
Persecuted to death	1
Situation not known	8
Total	58

The Post-Mao Period

After 1976 those who were wronged in the Cultural Revolution were gradually cleared. Moreover, the veterans of the Long March were again placed in high positions. Never before were so many women Long Marchers in such high positions. In 1979, thirty years after the establishment of the People's Republic of China, eleven women had become top leaders (admittedly some were honorary positions such as member of the Consultative Committee or the Discipline Inspection Committee of the Central Committee), twelve became high level cadres, six remained middle and low level cadres and two remained professionals. The number of retired increased to fifteen, while the number of deceased came to twelve. Table IX summarizes the position of the women in or around 1979.

TABLE IX
POSITION OF WOMEN IN 1979

POSITION	NUMBER
Top leadership	11
High level	12
Middle and low level	6
Professional	2
Retired	15
Dead	12
Total	58

After paying for a pear to give to her injured comrade, Xie Fei wrote a note to the absentee owner of the house. From Guo Chen, *Teshu liandui* (Nongcun duwu chubanshe, Beijing, 1985).

After the death of Zhang Qinqiu, Vice-Minister of the Textile Industry, another Vice-Minister emerged from the women veterans of the Long March. This was Jian Xianfo, who was appointed Vice-Minister of the Power Industry in 1979. Jian had kept a low profile thus far, but she was the wife of General Xiao Ke, and sister of Jian Xianren, General He Long's former wife. In 1978 Deng Yingchao became a full member of the powerful Politburo of the CCP Central Committee, the only woman (although Chen Muhua had been an alternate member) since Jiang Qing and Ye Qun to put her own name on its list, thereby creating an historical precedent in 1969. Deng and three other women became full members of the CCP Central Committee; one more became an alternate member and another became a member of its Discipline Inspection Committee. Four were on the Standing Committee of the National People's Assembly with Cai Chang and Deng Yingchao as Vice-Chairpersons. Four were also on the standing committee of the Political Consultative Conference, with Kang Keqing as its Vice-President.

The data after 1979 is not yet complete. However it is known that several more had died. He Zizhen, who was divorced from Mao Zedong in 1939, finally died in 1984 after a lonely forty-five years. She survived Mao and watched Jiang Qing, her persecutor, fall from power, be tried and condemned by law. Li Bozhao died in 1985, not before she completed her second major work, a play entitled *Northwards* which held its first performance in 1982, but missed out on becoming China's first lady when her husband Yang Shangkun became President a few years later in 1988.

Cai Chang retired from all positions before 1989 and died in 1990. Deng Yingchao hardly made any public appearances after June 1991. However, she was considered one of the Eight Elders—*Balao*—who were consulted on important affairs of state by the present regime. She died in May 1992. On her deathbed, she called for raising the discipline of Communist Party members.

In the 12th Central Committee of 1982 only two full members of the Central Committee were women Long Marchers, while none remained in the 13th Central Committee of 1987. Quite a few became members of the newly-established Consultative Committee of the Central Committee, and two of its Discipline Inspection Committee. Only one is on the National People's Assembly and three on the Standing Committee of the Political Consultative Conference, with Deng Yingchao as its President. Many more would have gone into retirement. From the above it may be concluded that the career of our heroines probably peaked in the late seventies and early eighties, after which it began to decline due to death and old age.

So far I have only analysed the work of the women vertically, that is, the level of the positions they reached. It should also be of interest to know the nature of their work, or at least the kind of institutions and organizations in which they were placed. Undoubtedly a majority of them held positions in the bureaucracy, in the party, the government or in the army. In China, the army has its own schools, hospitals, farms and so on, so that it employs a large number of bureaucrats. The departments in which the veteran women Long Marchers worked were quite diverse in nature.

Even among the party, government and army bureaucrats, some of the women have had more responsible jobs, such as head or deputy head of a department, section or division. Others have been office managers, and ordinary office workers. A couple of them who were married to very important men, became their confidential secretaries or what is now equivalent to executive assistants. Luo Ronghuan's wife Lin Yueqin, Liu Bocheng's wife Wang Ronghua, Dong Biwu's wife He Lianzhi and Ren Bishi's wife Chen Zongying fall into this category. We also find that they are scattered among the three different hierarchies of the party or of the government: central, provincial or local. Among the women we have one provincial party secretary, Li Jianzhen, Secretary of the CCP, Guangdong province, from 1960 to the Cultural Revolution and then from 1973 to 1979. At one time or another, almost all of them had been members of the representative organs such as the national, provincial and local people's assemblies and political consultative conferences. The most highly respected women in our group often devoted a great deal of their time to ceremonial roles and international public relations. Cai Chang, Deng Yingchao, Kang Keqing, Liu Ying and Zhang Qinqiu led various delegations to foreign countries, headed Friendship Societies with the Soviet bloc as well as some third world countries, in addition to working in peace organizations. They also headed or sat on committees to plan celebrations on occasions such as anniversaries of the October Revolution, the Chinese National Day and the commemorations of births or deaths of eminent historical figures such as Sun Yat-sen, Lu Xun, and Song Qingling.

Needless to say, they have also been found in the Women's Department of the various levels of government as well as the various levels of the Women's Federation. Cai Chang was the first President of the All-China Federation of Democratic Women (later All-China Federation of Women) and stayed in that position for thirty years, until 1979. From 1979 to 1988 she was Honorary President. Deng Yingchao and Zhang Qinqiu were among its first vice-presidents. Deng continued her work with the Women's Federation in the capacity of Honorary President until 1988, after which Kang Keqing took over the job of overseeing this national body. The Women's Federation and its provincial and local branches are powerful lobby groups in China. Both the first and the second marriage laws were born as a result of their efforts. Wherever there are law suits involving women, the Women's Federation would be there to see that women's rights were upheld.

Several of our women sat on the Committee for Implementing Marriage Laws. A more recent change in attitude, represented by a book on marriage and divorce in the PRC,[26] sees the Women's Federation's role of blindly trying to preserve marriages which had long since died as unnecessary and sometimes counterproductive. However, the economic reforms of the 1980s tend to return women to the relatively underprivileged position of before 1949, and hence, a national organization protecting the rights of women still seems needed, though perhaps its aims need also to be redefined in response to new social conditions.

The women were also asked to work with children, a role which may appear somewhat incongruous for those who had carried guns and fought in battles. For years Kang Keqing headed the Chinese People's Council for the Protection of Children, the Children's Welfare Department of the Women's Federation, National Co-ordinating Committee for Children, and Chinese Foundation for Children and Youth. Deng Liujin and Lin Yueqin were asked by their husbands to start nurseries for their army unit. A considerable number of the women have worked in the field of education. This is quite unexpected, in view of the fact that the education level of the group as a whole was not particularly impressive. These women served as heads (mostly deputy heads) of nursery schools, elementary and high schools, and tertiary and technical institutions. Their interest in nurseries, at least, was probably prompted by their own need for such facilities. Another popular field is health. Many of them had been orderlies and nurses during the war years, so this is perhaps not surprising. Some have worked in the health departments of the different levels of government and the military. Some have worked in hospitals and nursing homes as administrators or party officials. Several have been deputy directors of hospitals. Some of the women had experience in organizing labour movements before the Long March and during the Anti-Japanese War. After 1949 a few of them continued to work in these fields. Cai Chang was a member of the Presidium of the All-China Federation of Trade Unions. Others had positions in its local and industrial chapters.

In a socialist country, women and industry are not necessarily incompatible. We have mentioned above that two women had had industrial portfolios in the Central Government. They are Zhang Qinqiu, Vice-Minister of the Textile Industry from the birth of the People's Republic until the Cultural Revolution, and Jian Xianfo, Vice-Minister of the Power Industry from 1979. We also have two managers of factories. Nor is mining and geology unusual work for women. Several women worked in mining bureaux and geological institutes.

---

[26] Su Xiaokang, *Yin-yang da liebian.*

On the intellectual side, three women turned to writing. Li Bozhao has been mentioned earlier. Well known among her work is the opera, *The Long March,* in which Mao Zedong appeared for the first time as a stage character. Her swan song entitled *Northwards* is a play which depicts the conflict between Mao Zedong and Zhang Guotao before Mao emerged victorious to lead the Red Army north to fight the Japanese. Her other works include short stories, novels and many other plays. Ma Yixiang, the only Tujia national of our group, wrote a best seller in 1958 with the help of ghost writers. It not only did not bring her wealth (she donated every cent of her royalty, she said, to the party),[27] but brought her calamity during the Cultural Revolution. Her novel, *The Sunflower,* was classified as a great "poisonous weed", as it praised He Long. She was criticized in "struggle" sessions, her mother and younger brother who lived in the countryside of Hunan, far removed, it would appear, from the centre of power struggle, were persecuted to death. Liu Jian did not begin to write until after her retirement in 1973. Some of her works are deemed of sufficient high standard and importance to be included in the Chinese school curriculum. Like Ma Yixiang, her writing brought her trouble; she was attacked at "struggle" sessions for writing about Zhu De in her memoirs.

Some women have worked in the judicial branch of the government. Xie Fei, Liu Shaoqi's first wife, entered postgraduate law school at the mature age of thirty-nine. After her graduation she became the Deputy Principal of the Central School for Political and Legal Cadres. Two other women, Gan Tong and Wu Zhonglian, became Deputy-Director and Director of People's High Courts in Sichuan and Zhejiang respectively. Wang Dingguo, wife of the venerable Xie Juezhai, worked as the office manager of the People's Supreme Court's party committee, and later became Deputy Head of the Office of Judicial Administration. One of the women has worked in foreign affairs. Liu Ying whose husband Zhang Wentian was the first ambassador to the Soviet Union, was in charge of the party affairs of the Embassy. Later she was recalled by Zhou Enlai to be his assistant in the Foreign Ministry until her husband was condemned as a rightist.

Nursing one's ailing husband was also important work in the eyes of the party elders. Sometimes this work would be formally entrusted to the wife by the leadership. Ren Bishi's wife Chen Zongying, Luo Ronghuan's wife Lin Yueqin and Liu Bocheng's wife, Wang Ronghua, have all spent years of their lives taking care of their important husbands. After their husbands' deaths, they were rewarded with moderately high positions with few responsibilities. The ever-growing variety of workplaces also included hotels and guesthouses, libraries, agriculture departments, the national security department, the buying

---

station of a department store and the road maintenance section of a provincial department of communications.

In Conclusion

It has been said that very often in the beginning of a mass movement, when it is struggling to establish itself in a hostile environment, women are allowed to take more important roles; but as the movement grows stronger, the position of women in the movement gradually falls, until they are relegated to some general and low status work, or are expelled altogether. This situation seems to be more obvious in religious movements and political revolutions. Early Buddhist history in China reveals that some women enjoyed high esteem and others were allowed to play fairly important parts in the development of movements.[28] The Daoist religion is even more well known for the prominent role of women during the early stages of its existence.[29] As I study the lives of these women I cannot help but feel that there is some truth in this view.

Take the case of Kang Keqing. She had commanded combat troops before the Long March. During the Long March she did not stay with the other women, but marched with the regular army, sometimes carrying three or four rifles. She told Helen Snow that her ambition was to be an officer of the army. But instead, she was given many ceremonial roles and asked to work with children. Kang had no training in this field, while many other Chinese women had, and therefore she should have been able to perform better work in the army.

Kang Keqing is not the only example. Many other women who had combat experience were placed in civilian jobs. He Zizhen, Wei Xiuying, Wang Quanyuan, Li Zhen, Liu Liqing, Wu Shunying, Liu Jian, Guo Changchun, Yang Wenju and Zhang Qinqiu all fought under the Red Army banner, but Li Zhen is the only woman who has had a career in the military. One of them, Wu Shunying, retorted when her husband asked her to stay home and take care of the children, "Did I climb the Snowy Mountain and cross the Grassland just to take care of your children."[30] Yet that was exactly what was expected of her.

Deng Yingchao and Cai Chang were both highly intelligent women and had contributed a great deal to the cause of communism in China. But one has only to look at the positions they held to realize that they were mainly restricted to ceremonial roles and women's work. Even to the very end, when Deng was on the Central Committee or as a

---

[28] The lives of the nuns included in the *Biqiuni zhuan* are testament to this fact.

[29] Barbara E. Reed, "Taoism", *Women in World Religions*, pp. 174-80. Also, Sue Mackie, "Designer Daoism: Devout Men, Divine Women", paper presented at the 7th Biennial Conference of the Asian Studies Association of Australia, Australian National University, Canberra, 1988.

[30] Liaowang Bianjibu, *op. cit.*, p. 345.

member of the Eight Elders, she did not manage to contribute very much towards the policies of the government. On her deathbed, she voiced concern over the discipline problem of members of the Party. She had not been able to influence the Party or even to make her view more widely known before that.

Another point to make is that the fate of women is still always bound together with that of their husbands. During the Anti-Rightist Movement and the Cultural Revolution, all women whose husbands were attacked were also inevitably affected, no matter how innocent they themselves were. There seemed to be no need even to fabricate some crime for them; the fact that they were married to a criminal was sufficient cause to punish them. Yet the reverse is not always true. It seems that in socialist China, women have yet to gain a separate and thus independent identity from that of their husbands.

Helen Quach's Work With East and Southeast Asian Symphony Orchestras

Helen Quach, the world renowned orchestral conductor, was born in Saigon (Ho Chi Minh City), and raised by Vietnamese-Chinese parents. In spite of her totally Australian education and her glittering success in the Western world, she has devoted a great deal of her time to conducting orchestras in East and Southeast Asia. In communities where symphony music was little known, she helped to raise the interest level; in communities where orchestras were still in the fledgling stage, she contributed towards their development and upgrading; and in communities where orchestras already existed, she encouraged them to explore exciting new musical terrain. It is the purpose of this chapter to trace Quach's footsteps in this region and to attempt to assess the influence she has had on their symphony orchestras. Information for this paper was gleaned from the two interviews I had with Helen Quach, and from various printed sources, including an entry in an encyclopaedia of music, newspaper and journal articles, a slim volume of biography published in Taiwan, and also from concert programmes in Quach's own collection.

Born Guo Meizhen in 1940 to Vietnamese-Chinese parents, Helen Quach went to a French primary school in Saigon. Her father, Guo Rongtao, came from a family of businessmen which, at the time of her birth, was impoverished due to debts incurred by a great-uncle. Her mother, Zhou Yangzheng, also from a modest business family, was a kindergarten teacher. Her influence on Quach's career as a musician cannot be underestimated, as she was the prime moving force behind Quach's musical training. She herself had wanted to become a great pianist, but lacking the necessary conditions to accomplish her own ambition, she was determined to create those conditions for her daughter in whom she detected the same interest in music. With no knowledge of English and armed only with the promise of help from an Australian friend, Miss E. McDonough and her family, Zhou took her ten-year old daughter to Sydney. Quach finished schooling at a Brigidine convent at the age of fifteen and entered the New South Wales Conservatorium of Music, majoring in piano. During her years at the Conservatorium she also studied composition, history of music and orchestral music. She was especially interested in the biographies of composers which, she recalled later, helped her to understand the trials of every aspiring musician.

In her final year at the Conservatorium something happened which was to change her whole life. In 1959, Nicolai Malko, the resident conductor of the Sydney Symphony Orchestra, announced his intention to take apprentices who would study under the maestro with an Australian Broadcasting Commission scholarship. Quach had never considered being a conductor before. She applied because she thought learning to conduct would help her gain a more profound understanding of the music she was playing on the piano. After a series of gruelling tests, Quach was one of the six successful candidates, and only three remained in the programme after one year.

As Malko's protégée she had her first taste of conducting an orchestra. Her five public concerts won instant critical acclaim and marked the beginning of her career as a professional conductor. Unfortunately, Malko died in 1961, only one and a half years after Quach began her apprenticeship. His legacy to Quach was his books and notes on the techniques of conducting, which Quach found invaluable. Losing her Australian mentor, she began to look towards Europe for opportunities for learning and development. In the next three years she taught and saved in order to finance her European trip. Quach went to Italy in 1964 and studied under such masters as Carlo Zecchi, Sir John Barbirolli and Hermann Scherchen. During that year Quach began to take part in international competitions for conductors. She had not been asked to represent Australia. As she was travelling with a passport issued by the Republic of China from its embassy in Saigon, she wrote to the Ministry of Education in Taiwan and obtained credentials as a representative from the Republic of China. She did not succeed in gaining a place in the first two competitions she entered: the Dimitri Mitropolous International Music Competition for Conductors held in New York in 1964 and the Nicoli Malko Competition in Copenhagen in 1965.

Quach stepped onto Chinese soil for the first time when she was invited to visit Taiwan in 1965, together with a delegation of Italian trade and cultural personalities which included various Chinese musicians studying or working in Italy. She enjoyed a tremendous welcome from those whom she now considered her own people and among whom a thirst for music was growing. Apart from guest-conducting some of the orchestras, she was kept busy by requests from aspiring groups and individuals for her expert opinion and encouragement. Through contacts in Taiwan, she made guest appearances in Seoul and Houston. She also took part in the 7th International Conference of Music Education where she conducted the World Youth Orchestra. In 1967 when Quach entered the Mitropolous Competition for the second time, she won first prize. More important to her than the prize money was the one-year contract with the New York Philharmonic Orchestra, as assistant conductor to Leonard Bernstein. At the end of her engagement with the New York Philharmonic, she began a busy life as a guest-conductor. She travelled the world, covering all five continents and spent a large proportion of her time working in East and Southeast Asia. Soon after leaving New York she performed in Japan. In the same year she organized and trained a children's orchestra in Taiwan and toured with them around the island three times. In 1969 she took the children's orchestra to Manila to play at the opening of the Cultural Centre of the Philippines.

In 1971, during one of her frequent visits to her family in Australia, Quach decided to stay long enough to satisfy the requirement of the Immigration Department, and she became an Australian citizen. Making the most of her time in Australia, she founded the Kuring-gai Philharmonic Orchestra on the North Shore of Sydney.

On many occasions between 1968 to 1974 she conducted the Manila Symphony Orchestra; this led to her appointment as the Music Director of the Orchestra in 1974. One of the most significant achievements during her tenure there was the premiere of Leonard Bernstein's *Mass* in the Philippines. In 1975, International Women's Year, she made history as the first woman to conduct the San Francisco Symphony Orchestra.

Quach went to Hong Kong in 1976 to take up her appointment as resident Conductor of the Hong Kong Symphony Orchestra. Once more she directed her attention to educating young people by taking the orchestra to schools. In the same year she selected and trained the Hua-Mei Chamber Orchestra and took them on a tour of the United States as the bicentennial gift to the American people from the Republic of China. With the support of the business community of Taiwan, Quach founded her second symphony orchestra, the Taipei Philharmonic, in 1978. As the founder and Director/Conductor she had full control of the orchestra. This gave her an opportunity to put her own ideas to work. From its first concert in March 1979, the Taipei Philharmonic played to capacity audiences. Unfortunately, after one and a half years, local politics, financial difficulties and other factors caused the demise of the fledgling orchestra. However, she was soon appointed as resident Director of the government-supported Taiwan Provincial Symphony Orchestra.

In 1983 she became ill. Needing medical attention and total rest, she came back to Sydney and bought a house overlooking Sailor's Bay. Apart from treatment and rest, she also spent her time reading and studying operas, only occasionally conducting concerts. Although she had received a Western education, Quach inherited an interest in Chinese culture and thought.[1] In recent years she has shown a tendency towards introspection, as evidenced by her study of the philosophy of Laozi and Zhuangzi,[2] and her time spent in meditation.[3]

As a conductor, her colleagues and critics alike have given her excellent reviews. Being a woman in a predominantly man's field, she

---

[1] Gwen Robinson, "East and West in Harmony", *The National Times* (Canberra), April 1-7, 1983.

[2] Author's interview with Quach, June 1988.

[3] Audrey Denes, "Queen of Baton Finds a New Task: Opera Study Now a Big Part of Her Life", *North Shore Times* (Sydney), 30 March 1984.

could either be treated as a novelty or be discriminated against. Quite early in her career Bernstein said about her:

> Miss Quach runs the danger of being a pretty young woman, and thus conquering all hearts for non-musical reasons. But her performance as our assistant this season (1967-68) has given us reason to believe that she will succeed on musical grounds as well. Her rhythmic sense is sharp, her reflexes are quick, her address to the orchestra captivating. She seems to be at her best in works of large dimension (odd for so diminutive a creature), and if there is such a thing as a Maestra, Miss Quach could well be it.[4]

The above appraisal should eliminate all doubts about Quach's musical ability and quality. That she is exceptional can be borne out by this comment from Thor Johnson, a well known music educator:

> She has established herself as an extraordinary musical personality, fully capable of the enormous demands of a career as a major symphonic conductor. She is, indeed, a rarity among conductors.[5]

It is not clear whether Quach, a woman as well as an Asian, has been discriminated against in the world of Western music. However, it is a fact that while she has received extremely flattering reviews whenever she has conducted in Europe, North America and Australia, the only offers for long-term engagements have come from Asian countries, whose orchestras are still in early stages of development.

In 1988, recovering from an illness, Helen Quach began to look ahead again. She started seminars for soloists and choral groups, and the resulting work was broadcast by 2MBS FM, a Sydney radio station. She would also like to visit China and to work with orchestras there. "The best of my work," said Helen Quach in an interview in June 1988, "is still to come."[6]

After providing a brief account of Helen Quach's life and work to date as a backdrop, I can now proceed to discuss more specifically her work in East and Southeast Asia.

South Korea, Japan and Singapore

First, I would like to turn to the Asian countries with which Quach only had an intermittent association: South Korea, Japan and Singapore.

Quach's association with South Korea predates her winning the Mitropolous Prize. In 1966, while she was visiting Taiwan for the first time, the South Koreans learnt about her and invited her to Seoul. She later recollected that she was overwhelmed by the warm reception and hospitality showered on her by the South Korean people. She found

---

[4] "Quach: Dynamism Instead of Size", *Hong Kong Standard*, 29 May 1977.

[5] Thor Johnson's letter of recommendation for Helen Quach dated 26 August 1966.

[6] Author's interview with Quach, July 1988.

them more passionate than other East Asian peoples and hence it was comparatively easy to establish rapport with them both on a personal basis and musically. In comparison with other developing countries of the region, the orchestras were more advanced. The musicians were responsive to her directions, so that she was able to obtain the sound she wanted from them. James Wade, the music critic of the *Korean Times* comments, "Miss Quach... appears on the musical horizon with every prospect of becoming an established star in the orchestra firmament. In general, Miss Quach knows just what she wants from an orchestra and just how to get it."[7]

Although she had been invited to appear as guest-conductor for the Seoul Philharmonic, she was also asked to give two additional performances: one with the National Symphony of Korea and the other with the Seoul Women's String Orchestra. Since the latter mainly consisted of daughters of men in high social positions, and at that time it was considered improper for them to perform publicly, an "invitation only" concert was held in the ballroom of a big hotel. Quach was especially glad to work with them as she was always happy to see young people in Asia, especially young women, devote themselves to music. Quach returned to South Korea many times after that, including the occasion of the opening of its Cultural Centre in 1978, as guest-conductor for both the Seoul Philharmonic and the National Symphony.

When Quach returned to Asia in 1967, after fulfilling her contract with the New York Philharmonic, her first engagement was with the Tokyo Symphony Orchestra which has a long and distinguished history. At first she worked with the musicians through an interpreter, but she felt that the latter was not passing on the urgency of her directions. In her youth, Quach was known as the "female tyrant of the podium"—she was used to shouting and stamping her feet at her musicians when she was not getting the required effect.[8] Her interpreter would always turn her most dramatic demands into gentle entreaties. Consequently she dismissed her interpreter and conducted in English. The violence and power demanded by Shostakovitch's Symphony No. 5 were quite alien to the nature of the reserved, self-controlled and urbane Japanese. To get them to play with passion and abandonment was a long and hard struggle. Quach recalled that the musicians used to be so angered by her demands that they glared at her. However the final result was worth the drama. Marcel Grilli said in the *Japan Times*:

> The young Chinese conductor, Helen Quach, played at the Festival Hall by [i.e. to] a capacity audience. She made the Tokyo Symphony

---

[7] James Wade, "Woman Conductor Triumphs", *The Korean Times*, 25 February 1966.
[8] Author's interview with Quach, July 1988.

instrumentalists perform with spirit and alertness of attack and accentuation that I don't recall from these players for quite a long time.[9]

Even more complimentary was Klaus Pringsheim's review in the *Mainichi Daily News*:

> Wielding absolute authority over the Japanese musicians, she got from them the most completely satisfying performance I recall having ever heard of the Fifth Symphony by Shostakovitch, and she stood brilliantly any comparison in the Fifth Symphony by Tchaikovsky.[10]

Quach went with the Tokyo Symphony (playing the Tchaikovsky) on a sixteen concert tour of Japan. In some of the provincial cities she took so many curtain calls that organizers apologized to her for the trouble.

When the NHK Symphony Orchestra toured Taiwan in February 1971, Quach had the opportunity to lead this most prestigious Japanese orchestra. Its conductor, Hiroyuki Iwaki, took turns with Quach in conducting during the tour. He held her in high esteem and was impressed by her ability to make his orchestra produce a different sound after only a few rehearsals. Quach also conducted the Yomiuri Nippon Symphony Orchestra in 1967 and toured Hong Kong and Macau in December 1975 with the Tokyo City Symphony Orchestra. It was the first time a symphony orchestra had ever played in Macau. The Japanese love Western classical music. Their orchestras are well established and of high standard. Through her own interpretation of the music they played together and through shaping and creating the sound of the orchestra as she envisioned, Quach succeeded in putting her own personal imprint on the Japanese orchestras she conducted.

Helen Quach visited Singapore several times, the last time being in February 1983 as guest-conductor with the Singapore Symphony Orchestra.

The Philippines

Before her appointment as Music Director of the Manila Symphony Orchestra, Helen Quach had already played an important role in the development of this orchestra.[11] From 1968 to 1974 she conducted it in fourteen major symphony programmes and two Philippines concert tours. In addition, she donated her talents to the Luneta Free Concerts, performing ten times at the Rizal Park Auditorium. Being a perfectionist, Quach would not stop before she had obtained the desired result from her orchestra. An article by Rosalinda Orosa in the *Manila Chronicle* provides us with a glimpse of how Quach trained the Manila Symphony Orchestra. She describes Quach's infinite patience during

---

[9] Marcel Grilli, *Japan Times*, 23 August 1967.
[10] Klaus Pringsheim, *Mainichi Daily News*, 23 August 1967.
[11] Manila Symphony Society, *First Keynote Concert Program*, 30 August 1974.

Helen Quach conducting the Manila Symphony Orchestra in 1968.

rehearsals: once she devoted a full three-hour session to one movement; another time, two bars were repeated fourteen times. Possessing a keen ear she could detect an individual's minutest error in tune or tempo while the full orchestra was playing. Indeed, at every rehearsal, no musician escaped unscathed. To help the players, she would sing a particularly difficult passage to them, or she would come down from the podium, walk to the musician in question and mark his score personally.[12] Many Filipinos found that watching her rehearse was an experience in itself. At the conclusion of an unusually rousing finale, one observer exclaimed, "My hair stands on end." Another added, "I have never been so electrified [in] all my life."[13] Quach's rehearsals were attended regularly by all sorts of people—not just people connected with the orchestra, such as Mr and Mrs Benito Legarda, the patrons of the orchestra, who sat through many hours despite their busy schedule, but also piano teachers, music students and local conductors, who treated the rehearsals as learning sessions. "I learn so much by just watching Miss Quach," said one pianist. Three local conductors, each with a score in hand, followed Quach note by note.[14]

The Philippines celebrated the U.S. Bicentenary by giving a premiere performance of Leonard Bernstein's *Mass* in 1976. The American Embassy undertook to pay the royalty fee and have the three huge handwritten scores flown to Manila. It is a colossal work requiring an extensive orchestra, a jazz band and a street band. For this occasion Quach needed the combined sound of the Manila Symphony Orchestra and the Orchestra of the Cultural Centre of the Philippines. Local workers assisted in locating the additional bands and soloists. Quach recalled having particular trouble in finding a guitarist. While almost everyone in the Philippines played the guitar, it was not at all easy to find someone able to play the difficult beat of Bernstein's modern music.[15] This monumental effort marked the highlight of Quach's tenure in the Philippines.

Hong Kong

As with Manila, Helen Quach was invited to guest-conduct in Hong Kong before she was appointed resident Conductor of the Hong Kong Symphony Orchestra in 1976. She found the orchestra very uneven in standard, as it was in the process of changing from a semi-amateur orchestra to a professional one. She said in July 1976: "At the moment the orchestra still needs a great deal of training, especially training in technique, a lot of work must be done, because technique directly

---

[12] Rosalinda Orosa, "Helen Quach: A Woman Possessed", *Manila Chronicle*, 17 September 1968.
[13] *Idem.*
[14] *Idem.*
[15] Author's interview with Quach, July 1988.

affects the tone of the orchestra. I require all members to hear that symphonic 'sound', the sound."[16]

Quach was very active during the three years she was in Hong Kong. She performed at the opening of several Hong Kong Art Festivals and Asian Art Festivals as well as at regular concerts. These were well publicized affairs, often attended by British royalty. During this period she emphasized the importance of the education and development of young people. In an interview with a Hong Kong Chinese magazine she said:

It's a pity that all of those who learn music come from rich families. I really hope to set up some scholarships which will give poor students the opportunity to come in contact with orchestral music, and to have the opportunity to play classical music. Furthermore, I hope to encourage professional musicians to devote themselves to helping young people and nurturing new blood, so that symphony music can become popular in Hong Kong.[17]

To further this aim she took the Hong Kong Symphony to the young people of Hong Kong. It played at a number of high schools and demonstrated individual instruments so that the children could gain a better understanding of the tone and quality of each instrument and the part it played in a symphony orchestra as a whole. The schools responded warmly to this gesture. She also became involved with the City Philharmonic Orchestra. Unlike the Hong Kong Symphony Orchestra which was supported and administered by City Hall (the municipal government), the City Philharmonic was a community youth orchestra supported by Chinese businessmen. She explained in an interview the reason she was helping this amateur orchestra by pointing out the social responsibility of a musician. She believed that those who were endowed with talent should use it to help others:

By conducting this concert, I did not raise my prestige, on the contrary, in the eyes of the ordinary people, my prestige has even dropped. I did it also because I love young people. I find that young people here devote all their time to studying and working. They work very hard, but their spiritual life lacks in richness.... From all the members of the City Philharmonic, I not only require them to improve their technique, guide them to develop their talent, criticize their deficiencies, I also help them to overcome difficulties.... I also tell them: in concerts we don't just play music. Some famous musicians often play for money. After a while they will get tired of it. I tell them they play music together because music can bring people together. Music expresses our soul and feelings. When they are together, those who play better should help those whose standard is lower. Those with leadership should help other members of the

---

[16] Weng Huiyun, "Pingyi jinren, shuanglang leguan: yu Guo Meizhen yi xi tan", *Tupo*, No. 21, 15 July 1976, pp. 30-1.
[17] *Ibid.*, p. 30.

Orchestra. The City Philharmonic can also be viewed as a social scheme in which our social responsibilities are fostered....[18]

In the above quotations Quach reveals a genuine interest and concern for the young people in the community. Moreover, she stresses the importance of solidarity and mutual help in a new orchestra where not all members are of a high standard.

In 1978 an invitation came from Taiwan asking Quach to form a private symphony orchestra with the support of the Guotai Group, the largest local conglomerate. Quach took the offer and went to Taiwan.

Taiwan

When in 1965 Quach was invited to visit Taiwan for the first time, the standard of Western music was not very high. She conducted some of the orchestras there and listened to many aspiring groups and soloists. She was later invited to Tainan, a city which might be considered a cultural backwater of Taiwan, to listen to a children's orchestra organized by interested parents with the help of a teacher. She found, to her surprise, that it had promise. She left instructions and pledged to return the following year. This was the beginning of the Chinese Children's Symphony Orchestra. She returned every year as promised and trained the children. The following year she gave a concert with them in Tainan, and the third year she took them on tour round the island three times. Many cities on this tour had never heard a symphony orchestra before. Three years later, in 1969, Quach and her group were invited by Imelda Marcos to the Philippines to play at the opening of the Cultural Centre of the Philippines. The average age of the fifty-four member orchestra was twelve, some as young as eight. As it was the first time a children's group had made an overseas tour, they received a great deal of press coverage. Before they left for the Philippines, the Orchestra was asked to play at an orphanage sponsored by Madame Chiang Kai-shek, a performance attended by President Chiang and his wife.

In the Philippines, Quach and her children created a sensation: they had eight curtain calls. One newspaper reported that "If one closed his (sic) eyes while they played, one couldn't have guessed that this was an orchestra of boys in short pants and girls in bob hair, so adult was their mastery of their instruments and their notes."[19] In addition to the two performances for which they had been invited, they gave four more concerts and also played at the Marcos' palace. Quach herself was immensely proud of her children. Showing off photos of this visit in an interview many years later, she said to a reporter from a Hong Kong

[18] Bai Yunru, "Yishujia de shiming zaiyu biaoda zhen yu mei", *Guangjiaojing*, September 1977, p. 27.
[19] Alberto Corvera, "Kids' Orchestra Wins Adult Raves", *Philippine Times*, 20 September 1969.

magazine that seven thousand overseas Chinese and Filipinos were "moved to tears" during a concert.[20] It was said that after this historical visit of the children, people in Taiwan changed their views about music. Quach reported in an interview, "After this trip, even the butcher's children wanted to learn music."[21]

In a structured society such as Taiwan's, however, Quach often met with obstacles she did not expect and could not comprehend. For example, in 1970, she wanted to organize a music camp for young people of all ages. Everyone advised against it, because it broke with tradition. First of all, camps were traditionally organized either for primary students or for high school students. Quach's idea of a camp which included both groups made it difficult to apply for funds. Secondly, a camp for both boys and girls was unthinkable. Thirdly, music teachers guarded their students jealously, and they discouraged their students from playing with the students of other teachers. Consequently, some of the most promising young people did not participate. But despite all these obstacles, Quach had her camp and at the end of it the participants gave a successful concert which won great acclaim.

In 1976, Quach was invited by the Ministry of Education of Taiwan to form another children's orchestra. This time she chose thirty string players and, with the help of an excellent violin teacher, formed the Hua-Mei Chamber Orchestra, consisting mainly of high school students. The training took place on the campus of Tsinghua University during the summer vacation. During the U.S. Bicentenary, the orchestra made a 28-concert tour of eighteen states, as a gift from the Republic of China to the American people. They received very favourable reviews as can be seen by the following:

> The program performed Wednesday evening in Portland State University's superb Lincoln Hall Auditorium was one that any polished, professional string chamber orchestra might have played. There was no hint of condescension—toward the players or the audience. Conductor Helen Quach knew the 30 members of the Hwa-Mei Youth Chamber Orchestra from Taiwan, Republic of China, were equal to the rigorous program—she had prepared them. Never have I heard the sheer exuberant and absolute *joie de vivre* of Mozart... so vividly expressed as it was in the opening *Divertimenti* (sic) No. 1 in D Major under Ms Quach's direction. The same thorough attention to spirit and musical detail was manifested throughout the program....[22]

Once Quach told a reporter that she conducted Hua-Mei "because I feel Chinese children work very hard, have a good memory and are very

---

[20] Weng, *op. cit.*, p. 30.
[21] Author's interview with Quach, June 1988.
[22] Martin Clark, "Chinese Youth Excel under Helen Quach's Baton", *Oregon Journal,* 9 September 1976.

talented; they also have a special power of concentration."[23] It was quite obvious that she understood and loved the young people with whom she was involved.

Taiwan in the late 1970s began to enjoy the prosperity which now put her name among the "four little dragons" of Asia. A few private enterprises owned by Taiwanese people grew into huge conglomerates; among them was the Guotai Group which included businesses as diverse as plastic products and insurance. The directors of Guotai also had political ambitions—they were on friendly terms with top government officials interested in the arts, who persuaded them to support a private symphony orchestra, with Helen Quach in mind as director. Although Quach could speak Mandarin as well as Cantonese, she could not read or write fluently. These skills were considered necessary if she were to take up the directorship of the municipal or provincial orchestra, in order to deal with administrative directives and correspondence in Chinese. However, in a privately-sponsored orchestra, these obstacles could be easily overcome. Consequently, in 1978 the private Taipei Philharmonic Orchestra was formed, supported by the Guotai Group, with Quach as Director/Conductor.

The orchestra had over sixty people. Quach decided to bring in good musicians from overseas, America in particular, to lead each section of the orchestra and to help train those players with less experience. This was the realization of an idea which she had expressed more than once before, but it probably caused some discontent among the local musicians. When anti-American riots broke out with the news that the United States had recognized Mainland China, the Americans promptly left. The Orchestra had only performed one concert, and it had received overwhelming reviews. In spite of losing most of its lead players, the Taipei Philharmonic continued to fill the three thousand seat Guofu Jinian Guan (The Sun Yat-sen Memorial Hall) at every concert until its demise in 1980. The concerts were also televized and broadcast on radio. The media as a whole were captured by this unusual phenomenon and never tired of reporting on the activities of the Taipei Philharmonic.[24]

It is not clear why the Taiwan Philharmonic had to wind up. Some say that the Guotai Group had begun to have financial difficulties, and was reducing expenses. The costly symphony orchestra was the first victim.[25] Others say that local politics were involved.[26] Still others attribute the cause to a personality problem.[27] Whatever the reason, the fact remains that after all the hard work Quach had put in to establish

---

[23] Weng, *op. cit.*, p. 30.

[24] Author's interview with Quach, July 1988. This can also be seen in clippings from the Taiwan press of the period.

[25] Unsigned report, *Zhongguo shibao*, 7 January 1980.

[26] Author's interview with Quach, July 1988.

[27] Article by Tang Biyun, *Zhongguo shibao*, 7 January 1988.

Helen Quach was known for her rigorous demands on the orchestras she conducted, winning her the epithet "Tyrant of the podium".

it, this orchestra came to an end in 1980. After the premature end of the Taipei Philharmonic, concerned officials were anxious that Quach did not leave Taiwan. They believed that Taiwan needed someone of Quach's stature to help promote interest in classical music and to bring their orchestras to international standard. As a result, she was appointed resident Conductor of the Taiwan Provincial Symphony Orchestra in 1980; however, a bureaucrat remained to take charge of the administrative affairs. At this time younger players had already begun to play in the Taiwan Symphony and under Quach it continued to improve in standard. With it she made a successful tour of the island.

In 1983 she came back to Australia, sick and fatigued after a non-stop career of almost twenty years. Quach's association with Taiwan spanned almost two decades, from 1965 to 1983. Although she left it many times, her association with this country has been an enduring and close one. Apart from the orchestras mentioned above, she conducted many other choral groups and orchestras, such as the Taipei City Symphony Orchestra. She became widely known there, even to those who had nothing to do with music. She won honours such as a citation and a gold medal from the Ministry of Education, and was selected as one of the Ten Outstanding Young Women in 1966.

Quach faced some recurrent problems in her work with the orchestras of East and Southeast Asia. Firstly, because the people of the region viewed music as a form of entertainment, musicians were not ususally held in high regard. This did not provide much incentive for people to become musicians. Parents also worried about the unstable and insecure life a musician was likely to lead when they considered music as a career for their children. As a result, orchestras from the region often suffered from an imbalance caused by the lack of strong players in certain sections, especially wind instruments.

Secondly, some of the orchestras were still in a fledgling stage of development. As a result, conductors had to combat problems which were not within their professional duties, such as internal politics and official red tape. Having been brought up in Australia, Helen Quach was not familiar with the conventions and social conditions of Asian countries. Coupled with the lack of long-time local contacts, she could not deal with the business of the orchestra as smoothly as could a conductor who was born and bred in the local community. Consequently, a great deal of time and energy was unnecessarily wasted.

Despite these drawbacks, Helen Quach was able to make a considerable contribution towards orchestral music of the region. Firstly, in her work with orchestras in Singapore, South Korea, Hong Kong, Japan, the Philippines and Taiwan, Quach offered a variety of training. In some countries she demonstrated a dimension of music and a style of playing to which these countries were not accustomed. In others she helped to upgrade standards. To the orchestras of all of these countries she imparted her musical vision, her interpretation of the particular works being performed, the fruit of her thorough study of these works, and her inspiration. Quach said of herself that she was able to make lesser orchestras play with the "drama and big emotional canvas" of a world class orchestra.[28] Reviewers often commented on the different sound of an orchestra under her baton. People even benefited from attending her rehearsals, as demonstrated by Orosa's article.

Secondly, she has devoted herself to working with children and young people in the region. The children's orchestra, chamber orchestra and summer camp in Taiwan have provided training for many youngsters and given them the excitement of playing music together. Taking the Hong Kong Symphony Orchestra to high schools probably raised the interest level in music among the school students there. Her work has helped to foster generations of young musicians who, in the future, will become the backbone of the music community in these countries.

Thirdly, her own example of success in music, as well as the successful overseas tours she made with her orchestras, helped to change people's views about choosing music as a career. As a result, this has helped improve music education in these countries. Although people may still want their children to become doctors, accountants and lawyers, they are more willing than before to consider music as a career for them.

Fourthly, she took many orchestras on tour: around Japan twice, around Taiwan with NHK, the children's orchestra and the Taiwan Provincial; to Hong Kong and Macau with the Tokyo City Orchestra, and she toured the Philippines twice with the Manila Symphony. She introduced the orchestra to many people in smaller cities. Moreover, she gave many free concerts in parks so that people who would not normally go to concerts had the opportunity of hearing a symphony orchestra play. Hence she made a significant contribution towards the dissemination of orchestral music to the general population of the region.

---

[28] Author's interview with Quach, June 1988.

Glossary

A Xiang	阿香
Ada	阿大
An (Emperor)	安(帝)
An Lingshou	安令首
Ba Da	八達
Ba lao	八老
Ban Gu	班固
Ban You	班斿
Ban Zhao	班昭
Banpo	半坡
Bao Linghui	鮑令暉
Baochang	寶唱
Baxian lun	八賢論
biji xiaoshuo	筆記小説
Biqiuni zhuan	比丘尼傳
Bo Gu (Qin Bangxian)	博古(秦邦憲)
Cai Chang	蔡暢
Cao *dagu*	曹大家
Chang'an	長安
Chen (State)	陳(國)
Chen (Commandery)	陳(郡)
Chen, Lady	陳淑媛
Chen Changhao	陳昌浩
Chen Congying	陳琮英
Chen Dongyuan	陳東原
Chen Huiqing	陳慧清
Chen Muhua	陳慕華
Chen Qing	陳清
Chen Shaomin	陳少敏
Chen Zhenren	陳真仁
Chiang Kai-shek	蔣介石
Ching Hua	清華
Chu (State)	楚(國)
Cixi (Dowager Empress)	慈禧(太后)
Daolin	道林
Daorong	道容
Daoxing	道馨
Daoyi	道儀
Daozi	道子
Deng (Dowager Empress)	鄧(太后)

Deng Fa	鄧發
Deng Liujin	鄧六金
Deng Man	鄧曼
Deng Xiaoping	鄧小平
Deng Yingchao	鄧穎超
Deng Zhi	鄧騭
Di	氐
Ding Fubao	丁福保
Ding Ling	丁玲
Dong Biwu	董必武
Dong Hanhe	董漢河
Donghai	東海
Dongshan	東山
Duting	都亭
E	遏
Egu	阿谷
Ehuang	娥皇
Fashi	法式
Fei (River)	淝(水)
Feng	封
Fotu Cheng	佛圖澄
Fu Jian	苻堅
Fu Lianzhang	傅連璋
Furen ji	婦人集
Gan Tang	甘棠
Gaoseng zhuan	高僧傳
Gaozu	高祖
Gu	顧
Guangwu (Emperor)	光武(帝)
Guo (née)	郭(氏)
Guobao (Wang)	國寶(王)
Guo Changchun	郭長春
Guo Chen	郭晨
Guo Rongtao	郭榕滔
Guofu Jinian Guan	國父記念館
Guomindang	國民黨
Guotai	國泰
Guoxian	崞縣
Han Shiying	韓世英
Han Shizhong	韓世忠
Han shu	漢書
Han (dynsasty)	漢(朝)

He (Emperor)	和(帝)
He (Empress)	何(后)
He Chong	何充
He Hou	何后
He Lianzhi	何蓮芝
He Long	賀龍
He Yan	何晏
He Zhijian	賀志健
He Zizhen	賀子貞
Hongnong	弘農
Hou Han shu	後漢書
Hou Zheng	侯政
Hua Mulan	花木蘭
Huan Wen	桓溫
Huan Xuan	桓玄
Huangdi	黃帝
Huijiao	慧皎
Huizhan	慧湛
Ji (Nun)	濟(尼)
Jia (Empress)	賈(后)
Jian Xianfo	蹇先佛
Jian Xianren	蹇先任
Jiandi	簡狄
Jiang Qing	江青
Jiangling	江陵
Jiangyi	江乙
Jiangyuan	姜嫄
Jiangzhou	江州
Jianjing	簡靜
Jiankang	建康
Jianwen (Emperor)	簡文(帝)
Jianxing	建興
Jianyuan	建元
jie	節
Jin (dynasty)	晉(朝)
Jin shu	晉書
Jin Weiying	金維映
Jingjian	淨檢
Jinguo liezhuan	巾幗列傳
Jingzhou	荊州
Jiu Tang shu	舊唐書
juan	卷

Kan Siying	闞思穎
Kang (Emperor)	康(帝)
Kang Keqing	康克清
Kang Youwei	康有為
Kuaiji	會稽
Lang	朗
Langye	瑯琊
Lanzhou	蘭州
Laozi	老子
Lei (née)	雷(氏)
Li Bozhao	李伯釗
Li De	李德
Li Fuchun	李富春
Li Guiying	李桂英
Li Jian	李健
Li Jianhua	李建華
Li Jianzhen	李堅真
Li Qingzhao	李清照
Li Weihan	李維漢
Li Xiaojiang	李小江
Li Zhen	李貞
li	隸
Liang Hongyu	梁紅玉
Liang Qichao	梁啟超
Liao Shiguang	廖施光
Liao Siguang	廖似光
Liao Yuehua	廖月華
Lienü zhuan	列女傳
Liezong	列宗
Lin Yueqin	林月琴
Ling (Duke of Wei)	(衛)靈(公)
Ling (Emperor of Han)	(漢)靈(帝)
Lingzong	令宗
Lisao	離騷
Liu (Madam)	劉(夫人)
Liu Bang	劉邦
Liu Bocheng	劉伯承
Liu Caixia	劉彩霞
Liu Caixiang	劉彩香
Liu Dehan	劉德漢
Liu Jian	劉堅
Liu Ling	劉伶

Liu Liqing	劉立清
Liu Liu	劉柳
Liu Qunxian	劉群仙(先)
Liu Shaoqi	劉少奇
Liu Tao	劉濤
Liu Xiang	劉向
Liu Ying	劉英
Liu Yu	劉裕
Liu bo	六博
Loufan	樓煩
Lü (Empress)	呂(后)
Lü Kun	呂坤
Lu Xun (1)	魯迅
Lu Xun (2)	盧循
lüli zhi hui	閭里之會
Lun (née Ma)	(馬)倫
Lunyu	論語
Luo Fu (Zhang Wentian)	洛甫(張聞天)
Luo Ronghuan	羅榮桓
Luoyang	洛陽
Ma Bufang	馬步芳
Ma Rong	馬融
Ma Yixiang	馬憶湘
Mao Zedong	毛澤東
Mao Zemin	毛澤民
Meng Yi	孟覬
Mengji	孟姬
Miaoxiang	妙相
Miaoyin	妙音
Ming (dynasty)	明(朝)
Ming (Emperor)	明(帝)
Ming seng ji	名僧記
mingfu	命婦
Minggan	明感
Mingjia	名家
mingshi	名士
Mo	末
Mu (Emperor)	穆(帝)
Nanzi	南子
Neixun	內訓
Ning (Fan)	(范)寧
Nü fan jielu	女範捷錄

Nüjie	女誡
Nüwa	女媧
Nüxian waishi	女仙外史
Nüying	女英
Peng Dehuai	彭德懷
Qi (State)	齊(國)
Qi	棄
Qian Xijun	錢希鈞
Qin (State)	秦(國)
Qin Liangyu	秦良玉
Qing (dynasty)	清(朝)
qingtan	清談
Qiu Jin	秋瑾
Qiu Yihan	丘一涵
Quan jin shi	全晉詩
Quan Jin wen	全晉文
Ren Bishi	任弼時
renlun	人倫
Ruan Ji	阮籍
Ruijin	瑞金
Rulin zhuan	儒林傳
Sengji	僧基
Shangyu	上虞
Shen (Emperor of Ming)	(明)神(宗)
Shengping	升平
Shenqing fu	申情賦
Shi Hu	石虎
Shi Qunying	施群英
Shiji	史記
Shijing	詩經
Shishuo xinyu	世說新語
Shizhu	石柱
Shiziban	識字班
Shun	舜
si	寺
Sima Daozi	司馬道子
Sima Yue	司馬越
Sizhou	司州
Song Qingling	宋慶齡
Song Ruozhao	宋若昭
Soong (sisters)	宋(氏姊妹)
Sui shu	隋書

Sun En	孫恩
Sun Yat-sen	孫逸仙
Taikang	太康
Taiping	太平
Taiyuan	太原
Tanbei	曇備
Tang (dynasty)	唐(朝)
Tang Sai'er	唐賽兒
Tanluo	曇羅
Tonggong	通恭
tongsheng qi ren	同生七人
tongyangxi	童養媳
touhu	投壺
Tujia	土家
waisun	外孫
Wang (Lady)	王(夫人)
Wang Bi	王弼
Wang Chen	王忱
Wang Dao	王導
Wang Dingguo	王定國
Wang Dun	王敦
Wang Gong	王恭
Wang Lan	王覽
Wang Ningzhi	王凝之
Wang Qianyuan	王乾元
Wang Qiao	王喬
Wang Quanyuan	王泉媛
Wang Rong	王戎
Wang Ronghua	汪榮華
Wang Tanzhi	王坦之
Wang Xiang	王祥
Wang Xianzhi	王獻之
Wang Xizhi	王羲之
Wang Yan	王衍
Wei (King of Qi)	(齊)威(王)
Wei (Lady)	衛(夫人)
Wei (State)	衛(國)
Wei Gongzhi	危拱之
Wei Xiuying	危秀英
Wei Zifu	衛子夫
Wei-Jin	魏晉
weina	維那

Wu (Emperor of Han)	(漢)武(帝)
Wu (Empress)	武(后)
Wu (King of Chu)	(楚)武(王)
Wu Fulian	吳富蓮
Wu Hulian	吳胡蓮
Wu Zhonglian	吳仲連(廉)
Wuxi	無錫
Xi Kang	嵇康
Xi'an	西安
Xiang Jingyu	向警予
Xiao (Duke of Qi)	(齊)孝(公)
Xiao Ke	蕭克
Xiaowu (Emperor)	孝武(帝)
Xie An	謝安
Xie Daoyun	謝道韞
Xie Fei	謝飛
Xie Heng	謝衡
Xie Jing	謝靖
Xie Ju	謝據
Xie Juezhai	謝覺齋
Xie Kang	謝康
Xie Kun	謝鯤
Xie Lang	謝朗
Xie Pou	謝裒
Xie Quan	謝泉
Xie Shang	謝尚
Xie Shao	謝韶
Xie Shi	謝石
Xie Tie	謝鐵
Xie Wan	謝萬
Xie Wuliang	謝無量
Xie Xiaomei	謝小眉(梅)
Xie Xuan	謝玄
Xie Yan	謝琰
Xie Yi	謝奕
Xilujun nüzhanshi mengnan ji	西路軍女戰士蒙難記
Xin Tang shu	新唐書
Xishi	西施
Xu (Empress)	徐(皇后)
Xu Haidong	徐海東
Xu Xun	許詢
Xuanxue	玄學

Xunyang	潯陽
ya	雅
Yan Kejun	嚴可均
Yan Ying	晏嬰
Yan'an	延安
Yang Guifei	楊貴妃
Yang Houzeng	楊厚增
Yang Houzhen	楊厚珍
Yang Shangkun	楊尚昆
yang	陽
Yangxia	陽夏
Yanmen	雁門
Yanxing	延興
Yao	堯
Ye Jianying	葉劍英
Ye Qun	葉群
Yijing	易經
Yin Hao	殷浩
Yin Zhongkan	殷仲堪
yin	陰
Yishao (Wang)	(王)逸少
Yiwen leiju	藝文類聚
Yixing	義興
youxian shi	遊仙詩
Yu	庾
yu	御
Yuan Mei	袁枚
Yuan Yuezhi	袁悅之
yuefu	樂府
Yuzhou	豫州
Zeng Xianzhi	曾憲植
Zeng Yu	曾玉
Zhang Guotao	張國燾
Zhang Qinqiu	張琴秋
Zhang Wentian	張聞天
Zhang Xuan	張玄
Zhao (King of Chu)	(楚)昭(王)
Zhao Feiyan	趙飛燕
Zheng Yu	鄭玉
Zhi (née Ma)	(馬)芝
Zhi Miaoyin	支妙音
Zhishan	智山

Zhisheng	智勝
Zhixian	智賢
Zhong jing mulu	眾經目錄
Zhong Shanfu	仲山甫
Zhong Yuelin	鍾月林
Zhong Yulin	鍾玉林
Zhongguo funü shenghuo shi	中國婦女生活史
Zhongguo funü	中國婦女
Zhonglang	中郎
Zhongxing shu	中興書
Zhongyong	中庸
Zhou (Duke of)	周公
Zhou (dynasty)	周(朝)
Zhou Enlai	周恩來
Zhou Yangzheng	周仰正
Zhou Yuehua	周越華
Zhu Daoxing	竺道馨
Zhu De	朱德
Zhuangzi	莊子
Zhuge Liang	諸葛亮
Zhulin	竹林
zhuzi	諸子
Zigong	子貢
Zuan	纘
Zunyi	遵義
Zuo Fen	左芬
Zuo zhuan	左傳

Bibliography

Ayscough, Florence, *Chinese Women Yesterday and Today* (Jonathan Cape, London, 1938).

Bai Yunru, "Yishujia de shiming zaiyu biaoda zhen yu mei", *Guangjiaojing* (September, 1977), pp. 24-8.

Barnes, Nancy Schuster, "Buddhism", Arvind Sharma (ed.), *Women in World Religions* (State University of New York, 1987), pp. 105-59.

Beahan, Charlotte, "Feminism and Nationalism in the Chinese Women's Press, 1902-1911", *Modern China*, Vol. 1, No. 4 (1975), pp. 379-417.

Biqiuni zhuan in *Dazang jing*, Binga sheishu ed.

Chen Dongyuan, *Zhongguo funü shenghuo shi* (Shangwu yinshuguan, Shanghai, 1937).

Cissell, Kathryn Ann Adelsperger, "The *Pi-ch'iu-ni chuan*: Biographies of Famous Chinese Nuns from 317-516 CE" (Ph. D. thesis, University of Wisconsin, 1972).

Clark, Martin, "Chinese Youth Excel Under Helen Quach's Baton", *Oregon Journal*, 9 September 1976.

Corvera, Alberto, "Kids' Orchestra Wins Adult Raves", *Philippine Times*, 20 September 1969.

Denes, Audrey, "Queen of Baton Finds a New Task: Opera Study Now a Big Part of Her Life", *North Shore Times* (Sydney), 30 March 1984.

Dong Hanhe, *Xilujun nüzhanshi mengnan ji* (Jiefangjun wenyi chubanshe, Beijing, 1990).

Dull, Jack, "Marriage and Divorce in Han China: a Glimpse at 'Pre-Confucian' Society", David C. Buxbaum, *Chinese Family Law and Social Change: In Historical and Comparative Perspective* (University of Washington Press, 1978), pp. 23-74.

Fang Jucheng and Fang Guinong, *Zhou Enlai: A Profile by Percy Jucheng Fang and Lucy Guinong J. Fang* (Foreign Languages Press, Beijing, 1986).

Frost, Molly Spitzer, *Chinese Matriarchy: Clues from Legends and Characters* (Ph. D thesis, Georgetown University, 1982).

Gao seng zhuan in *Dazang jing*, Binga seishu ed.

Gipolon, Catherine, "The Emergence of Women in Politics in China, 1898-1927", *Chinese Studies in History* (Winter 1989/90), pp. 46-67.

Grilli, Marcel, *Japan Times*, 23 August 1967.

Guisso, Richard W. and Stanley Johannesen (eds), *Women in China: Current Directions in Historical Scholarship* (Philo Press, Youngstown, 1981).

Guo Chen, *Jinguo liezhuan: hong yifangmian jun sanshi wei changzheng nü Hongjun shengping shiji* (Nongcun duwu chubanshe, Beijing, 1986).

Guo Moruo, *Zhongguo gudai shehui yanjiu* (Renmin chubanshe, Beijing, 1974).

Gushi jishi deng sizhong (3rd printing; Shijie shuju, Taipei, 1978).

Han shu (Zhonghua shuju, Beijing, 1962).

Hou Han shu (Zhonghua shuju, Beijing, 1965).

Huaxia funü mingren cidian (Huaxia chubanshe, Beijing, 1988).

Klein, Donald and Anne Clark (eds), *Biographic Dictionary of Chinese Communism, 1921-1965* (Harvard University Press, 1971).

Jin shu (Zhonghua shuju, Beijing, 1974 and 1984).

Li Ruzhen, *Jing hua yuan* (Zhonghua shuju, Hong Kong, 1958).

Li Xiaojiang, *Xiawa de tansuo* (Henan renmin chubanshe, Zhengzhou, 1988).

Liaowang Bianjibu (ed.), *Hongjun nüyingxiong zhuan* (Xinhua chubanshe, Beijing, 1986).

Lienü zhuan, TSCC, no. 3400.

Liu Dehan, *Dong Zhou funü shenghuo* (Xuesheng shuju, Taipei, 1965).

Liu Yiqing, *Shishuo xinyu jiaojian*, ed. by Yang Yong (Dazhong shuju, Hong Kong, 1969).

Lü Xiong, *Nüxian waishi* (Baihua wenyi chubanshe, Tianjin, 1985).

Lunyu, SPPY ed.

Mackie, Sue, "Designer Daoism: Devout Men, Divine Women", paper presented at the 7th Biennial Conference of the Asian Studies Association of Australia, Australian National University, Canberra, 1988.

Manila Symphony Society, *First Keynote Concert Program*, 30 August 1974.

Mao Zedong, *Mao Zedong xuanji* (Beijing renmin chubanshe, 1977).

Maoshi zhengyi, SPPY ed.

Martin-Liao, Tienchi, *Frauenerziehung im Alten China, eine Analyse der Frauenbücher* (Brockmeyer, Bochum, 1984).

Ming shi (Zhonghua shuju, Beijing, 1974).

O'Hara, Albert Richard, *The Position of Women in Early China According to the Lieh Nü Chuan, "The Biographies of Chinese Women"* (Mei Ya Publications, Taipei, 1971).

Orosa, Rosalinda, "Helen Quach: A Woman Possessed", *Manila Chronicle*, 17 September 1968.

Perrot, Michel, *et al.*, "A propros du destin de la femme XVIe au XXe siècle", Evalyn Sullerot (ed.), *Le Fait feminin* (Fayard, Paris, 1978), pp. 425-45.

Pringsheim, Klaus, *Mainichi Daily News*, 23 August 1967.

Qin Liangyu shiliao jicheng (Sichuan daxue chubanshe, Chengdu, 1987).

Qiu Zhizhuo, *Zhonggong dangshi renminglu* (Chongqing chubanshe, Chongqing, 1986).

"Quach: Dynamism Instead of Size", *Hong Kong Standard*, 29 May 1977.

Reed, Barbara E., "Taoism", *Women in World Religions* (State University of New York Press, Albany, 1987), pp. 174-80.

Robinson, Gwen, "East and West in Harmony", *The National Times* (Canberra), April 1-7, 1983.

Ropp, Paul S., "The Seeds of Change: Reflections on the Conditions of Women in the Early and Mid Ch'ing", *Signs*, No. 2, 1976, pp. 5-23.

Ropp, Paul S., *Dissent in Early Modern China* (University of Michigan Press, 1981).

Salisbury, Harrison E., *The Long March: The Untold Story* (Harper and Row, New York, 1985).

Shiji (Zhonghua shuju, Beijing, 1959).

Shishuo xinyu jiaojian. See Liu Yiqing.

Smedley, Agnes, *The Great Road* (Monthly Review Press, New York, 1956).

Snow, Edgar, *Red Star Over China* (1st revised and enlarged ed; Penguin, New York, 1968).

Snow, Helen Foster, *Chinese Communists: Sketches and Autobiographies of the Old Guards* (Greenwood, Westport, 1972).

Snow, Helen Foster, *Women in Modern China* (Mouton, The Hague, 1967).

Song shi (Zhonghua shuju, Beijing, 1977).

Song shu (Zhonghua shuju, Beijing, 1974).

Su Xiaokang, *Yin-yang da liebian* (Nanyue chubanshe, Hong Kong, 1989).

Sui shu (Zhonghua shuju, Beijing, 1977).

Swann, Nancy Lee, *Pan Chao: Foremost Woman Scholar of China, First Century A.D.* (Century, New York, 1932).

Tang Biyun, *Zhongguo shibao*, 7 January 1988.

Tang Qiu, *Jin yangqiu jiben*, TSCC, no. 3805.

Ts'ai, Kathryn Ann, "The Chinese Buddhist Monastic Order for Women: the First Two Centuries", Richard W. Guisso and Stanley Johannesen (eds), *Women in China: Current Directions in Historical Scholarship* (Philo Press, Youngstown, 1981), pp. 1-20.

van Gulik, Robert, *Sexual Life in Ancient China: a Preliminary Survey of Chinese Sex and Society from 1500 B.C. to 1644 A.D.* (E. J. Brill, Leiden, 1961).

Wade, James, "Woman Conductor Triumphs," *The Korean Times*, 25 February 1966.

Wolf, Margery and Roxane Witke (eds), *Women in Chinese Society* (Stanford University Press, 1975).

Weng Huiyun, "Pingyi jinren, shuanglang leguan: yu Guo Meizhen yi xi tan", *Tupo*, No. 21, 15 July 1976, pp. 30-1.

Williams, E. T., *China Yesterday and Today* (4th ed; Crowell, New York, 1927).

Wilson, D., *The Long March, 1935: The Epic of Chinese Communism's Survival* (Hamilton, London, 1971).

Xi zhongsan ji, SPPY ed.

Xi'an Banpo Bowuguan (comp.), *Zhongguo yuanshi shehui* (Wenwu chubanshe, Beijing, 1977).

Xie Wuliang, *Zhongguo funü wenxueshi* (Zhonghua shuju, Shanghai, 1916).

Yan Kejun, *Quan Jin wen*, 1894.

Young, Marilyn, *Women in China: Studies in Social Changes and Feminism* (Center for Asian Studies, Ann Arbor, 1973).

Zhonggong dangshi renwu zhuan (Shaanxi renmin chubanshe, Xi'an, 1980-).

Zhonggong renming lu (International Relations Research Institute of the Republic of China, Taipei, 1967).

Zhu Lifu, *Erwan wuqian li changzheng ji* (Kangzhan chubanshe, Shanghai, 1938).

Zhuangzi, SPPY ed.

Zuo zhuan, SPPY ed.

WILD PEONY PTY LTD BOOK PUBLISHERS
A.C.N. 002 714 276
PO BOX 636 BROADWAY NSW 2007 AUSTRALIA
Fax: 61 2 566 1052

EXCEPTING TITLES MARKED WITH ASTERISK: International Distribution: University of Hawaii Press, 2840 Kolowalu Street, Honolulu Hawaii 96822. Fax: 1 808 988-6052

• *Shijin: Autobiography of the Poet Kaneko Mitsuharu, 1895-1975.* Introduction and Translations by A. R. Davis; edited by A. D. Syrokomla-Stefanowska. University of Sydney East Asian Series, No. 1; ISBN: 0 9590735 3 1; 1988; 324pp; hardcover: AUS $40.00

* Tanizaki Jun'ichiro, *A Cat, Shozo and Two Women.* Translated by Matsui Sakuko. University of Sydney East Asian Series, No. 2; ISBN: 0 9590735 5 8; 150pp; 1988; hardcover: AUS $27.95; softcover: AUS $12.95. NOT FOR SALE IN THE USA, CANADA AND UK.

• Yang Lian, *Masks and Crocodile: A Contemporary Chinese Poet and His Poetry.* Introduction and Translations by Mabel Lee; 12 coloured illustrations by Li Liang. University of Sydney East Asian Series, No. 3; ISBN: 0 9590735 7 4; 1990; 146pp; softcover: AUS $25.00

• *Gen'ei: Selected Poems of Nishiwaki Junzaburo, 1894-1982.* Translations by Yasuko Claremont. University of Sydney East Asian Series, No. 4; ISBN: 0 9590735 8 2; 1991; 120pp; softcover: AUS $19.95

• *Seven Stories of Modern Japan.* Edited by Leith Morton. Translations by H. Clarke, S. Matsui and L. Morton. University of Sydney East Asian Series, No. 5; ISBN: 0 9590735 9 0; 1991; 88pp; softcover: AUS $19.95

• *Kyunyŏ-jŏn: The Life, Times and Songs of a Tenth Century Korean Buddhist Monk.* Translated and annotated by Adrian Buzo and Tony Prince. University of Sydney East Asian Series, No. 6; ISBN: 0 646 14772 2; 1993; 142pp; softcover: AUS $25.00

• *Modernity in Asian Art.* Edited by John Clark. University of Sydney East Asian Series, No. 7; ISBN: 0 646 14773 0; 1993; 350pp; softcover: AUS $37.50

• *The Chinese Femme Fatale.* Short Stories of the Ming Period. Translations by Anne McLaren. University of Sydney East Asian Series, No. 8; ISBN: 0 646 14924 5; 1994; softcover: AUS $22.95